HOW TO WRITE
PERSUASIVELY TODAY

HOW TO WRITE PERSUASIVELY TODAY

Carolyn Davis

Writing Today

 GREENWOOD

AN IMPRINT OF ABC-CLIO, LLC
Santa Barbara, California • Denver, Colorado • Oxford, England

Library of Congress Cataloging-in-Publication Data
Davis, Carolyn.
    How to write persuasively today / Carolyn Davis.
        p. cm. — (Writing today)
    Includes bibliographical references and index.
    ISBN 978-0-313-37837-9 (alk. paper) — ISBN 978-0-313-37838-6 (ebook)
1. English language—Rhetoric—Study and teaching. 2. Persuasion (Rhetoric)—
Study and teaching. 3. Report writing—Study and teaching. I. Title.
    PE1431.D38   2010
    808'.042071—dc22   2009048643

ISBN: 978-0-313-37837-9
EISBN: 978-0-313-37838-6

14   13   12   11   10   1   2   3   4   5

This book is also available on the World Wide Web as an eBook.
Visit www.abc-clio.com for details.

Greenwood
An Imprint of ABC-CLIO, LLC

ABC-CLIO, LLC
130 Cremona Drive, P.O. Box 1911
Santa Barbara, California 93116-1911

This book is printed on acid-free paper ∞

Manufactured in the United States of America

To common sense and moderation

CONTENTS

SERIES FOREWORD

Writing is an essential skill. Students need to write well for their coursework. Business people need to express goals and strategies clearly and effectively to staff and clients. Grant writers need to target their proposals to their funding sources. Corporate communications professionals need to convey essential information to shareholders, the media, and other interested parties. There are many different types of writing, and many particular situations in which writing is fundamental to success. The guides in this series help students, professionals, and general readers write effectively for a range of audiences and purposes.

Some books in the series cover topics of wide interest, such as how to design and write web pages and how to write persuasively. Others look more closely at particular topics, such as how to write about the media. Each book in the series begins with an overview of the types of writing common to a practice or profession. This is followed by a study of the issues and challenges central to that type of writing. Each book then looks at general strategies for successfully addressing those issues, and it presents examples of specific problems and corresponding solutions. Finally, each volume closes with a bibliography of print and electronic resources for further consultation.

Concise and accessible, the books in this series offer a wealth of practical information for anyone who needs to write well. Students at all levels will find the advice presented helpful in writing papers; business professionals will value the practical guidance offered by these handbooks; and anyone who needs to express a complaint, opinion, question, or idea will welcome the methods conveyed in these texts.

PREFACE

What is the function of a persuasive essay? How does it differ from other types of essays?

A persuasive essay is an intellectual argument that presents a point of view. The main difference between a persuasive essay and other types of essays is that it relies principally on effective argument to sway readers to a particular point of view. The essay or presentation often incorporates facts and quotations as backup. This book is an instruction manual in the techniques and true art of writing to persuade.

Persuasion is a skill that many beings, not only humans, use from infancy. As Aristotle observed, the main difference between humans' and other animals' forms of persuasion is that from an early age humans are expected to develop many of our inspirations, growth experiences, investigations, passions, research, and arguments in writing. We are all convinced of the validity and logic of our positions—or, at least, we may have to convince others that our position is correct. How do we influence readers and audiences effectively? That is what this guide seeks to answer, using practical methods and tips for presenting points of view or arguments in writing, based principally on my experiences during 20 years as a writer and 30-plus as a public speaker. Other references include excerpts from written material from other persuasive folks: teachers, authors, conflict theorists, and businesspeople.

This work is focused on a large segment of the population. The chapters are divided into subheadings and discuss how and why to write persuasively. Examples of problems and solutions in a variety of formats of written presentations and ways to deal with them are discussed, and a brief analysis of the concept of power is provided. The economist and historian Kenneth Boulding wrote that power tends to be hierarchical in groups, and decision-making roles develop. Boulding also argued that "hierarchical power cannot survive unless it can be legitimated. Authority in some sense is always granted from below,"[1] which in a writer's case can be interpreted as a group of readers granting writers' authority to promote their views and proposals in a public forum. This book guides you through the process of presenting your views, including such important concepts as how to structure a persuasive essay for school, how to reach across a language barrier, how to handle cultural differences, and some strategies to be aware of in environments of disagreement. The last two should be of particular use to professionals, but all of the topics can be helpful to persuasive writers in high school, college, graduate school, or the workplace.

The guide begins with a chapter entitled "What Am I Writing?," which is an overview of persuasive writing: what it is; the forms it takes, and how it is incorporated into academic and professional writing. The chapter also describes different styles of persuasive writing and how they can be used to suit different purposes and moods and an author's personal preference.

"Issues and Challenges" are presented next, including how to establish credibility as an authority, or at least someone who has researched the topic, with your readers or audience; how not to be boring; and how to relate to your readers and convince them to care about your perspectives by explaining why you have your particular points of view and why your perspectives should be important to your audience. Aspects of persuasive significance include the importance of knowing key words and phrases relating to your area, be it a research topic, a professional situation, or another culture or a pairing of two or a combination of all three. This section includes situations and issues that may influence or clog the author's objectivity and authority and options that can lead to resolutions. Examples of first-person reporting are provided: a peace conference in Turkey during which I, a woman who is disabled, experienced harassment along with a self-identified "half-Turkish and half-Kurdish" speaker and a presenter who spoke of the Armenian genocide of 1917. The latter two risked arrest to present their perspectives in a public forum. Other examples include deadline anxiety and writer's block. Excerpts from speeches by the former British prime minister Tony Blair and President Barack Obama are compared for particular points of persuasiveness. A section about the differences between what is known versus what is interpreted contains two historical references. One is my research about Wales in the Middle Ages, which demonstrates how historical facts can be interpreted. The other is recent history of the Native Americans' occupation of Wounded Knee, South Dakota, in 1972 and is an excerpt from an interview with some of the participants.[2] Excerpts from my presentations and essays are included. The chapter also presents the structure of an analytical outline, a fictitious letter requesting an appeal of a dissertation decision, and an "appeal to the emotions," followed by an essay of a cooperative human-feline rescue.

Next is the chapter "Problems and Solutions," which cites some major problems, beginning with plagiarism, redundancy, and hostile or apathetic audiences—how to avoid, anticipate, and deal with these problems. The chapter also addresses writers' and speakers' attitudes and provides some examples of problems and solutions within the larger framework of writers' and presenters' public lives. The heading, "What Frightens You? Confronting Personal and Professional Demons" includes excerpts from Elie Wiesel's and the late Hugh Gallagher's autobiographies as examples of authors' writing about extreme personal challenges. Additionally, there are examples from my own essays. The section about hostile or apathetic audiences includes excerpts from biographies of Angelina and Sarah Grimké, abolitionists and feminist speakers from the 19th century. A survey is used as an example of a method of information collection and presentation, and there are sections on writing proposals and prospectuses, strategies for completing work on time, and persuading colleagues, with examples from motion study pioneers Frank B. Gilbreth and Dr. Lillian M. Gilbreth, an excerpt from an interview with attorney Alan Dershowitz, which was conducted by Diane Cyr and became an appendix to *Why We Must Run with Scissors*,[3] and an example from one of my recent presentations.

Following logically from "Problems and Solutions" is the chapter "Strategies for Success," which begins with the subheading, "Everything that Attracted Me to Reading Reports for School, College, and Business I Learned by the Fourth Grade." Included is what makes a successful report and what authors should become aware of during the research and writing process: are the authors well informed not only about their topics, but also about their readers and what strategies, structures, and topic choices are appropriate. Strategies for avoiding arrogance and persuading instead of bullying are also included. The examples cited include political speeches; biographical sketches; religious texts; a survey; a resume; and references to grant, business, and book proposals. Additional strategies are discussed, and examples of a cover letter, links to online resources for students, a discussion of the positive outcome of a story, and an example of the use of satire to make a point are provided.

Included throughout the text are fictitious humorous examples of persuasive writing, including a letter imploring the purchase of a pair of noisy shoes by a minister and an advertisement extolling the multiple virtues of Sloppo soap. Many Web pages are mentioned as resources, including those that describe and demonstrate structures of persuasive essays to address more serious topics, outline grant proposals from venture capitalists, or provide exercise and relaxation techniques to avert or dissolve writer's block.

The guide finishes by identifying resources for the future in an annotated bibliography. Included are print and electronic resources for persuasive writing.

Much of the impact of a successful essay or presentation depends on its focus. As you prepare your persuasive strategy, ask yourself any or all of these questions as appropriate: In the context of this essay, article, or presentation, what do my readers want? What do they fear? What experiences are common to my readers? What do they expect from me and how should I present it? The answers to these questions can be your starting points, and your transitional paragraphs are major facilitators in how you address these issues.

NOTES

1. Kenneth E. Boulding, *Three Faces of Power* (Newbury Park, CA: Sage, 1989), 44.

2. American Experience, *We Shall Remain: Wounded Knee*, 24, www.pbs.org/wgbh/amex/weshallremain/files/transcripts/WeShallRemain_5_transcript.pdf.

3. Barry Lane and Gretchen Bernabei, *Why We Must Run With Scissors: Voice Lessons in Persuasive Writing 3–12* (Shoreham, VT: Discover Writing Press, 2001).

ACKNOWLEDGMENTS

I extend thanks to people who have been influential during the development and writing of this book. I give particular thanks to Carol Smallwood, editor of *Thinking Outside the Book: Essays for Innovative Librarians* and many other works, a prolific writer, poet, and editor, for bringing my name to the attention of George Butler of ABC-CLIO, and to George Butler himself. Additionally, I owe a tremendous debt of thanks to Cynthia Brackett-Vincent, publisher/editor of the *Aurorean* poetry journal. To Carol and Cynthia thanks also for permission to use a different version of an excerpt from a vignette that is a part of an anthology of theirs (*Contemporary American Women: Our Defining Passages*); sincere appreciation to a gifted historian and author, Mark H. Dunkelman; Kim Shafer, English teacher, editor, and friend, who "babysat" a copy of the manuscript for safe keeping throughout its development. To Steve Davies, editor and publisher of *Endangered Species and Wetlands Report*, who proofread and made suggestions about parts of the text. Kathleen Garrity, who was and is benign but honest in criticism and friendship; Dina Witwicki, my friend and a gifted persuader; Sheila Intner, dean emerita of the Mount Holyoke campus of the Simmons GSLIS; and Daniel O'Connor, attorney. I extend particular thanks to the Reverend Elizabeth A. Vincent, for her permission to use excerpts from her sermon, "The Image of God," and to editor Maxine Williams, a gifted writer and friend, who went beyond the call of friendship to assist me with the guide's index and proofread the entire text. I should like to thank writer and university lecturer Katie W. Berg, insightful Nate J. Berg, writer and editor Noah E. Davis, and friends Nancy Poor and Brian Patch for the assistance that each gave to me at various times during this manuscript's development.

Finally, I would like to extend my appreciation to the memory of my mother, Elizabeth W. Davis, who loved language and rational persuasive arguments.

CHAPTER 1

What Am I Writing?

Literature . . . is an Art rather, the success of which depends on personal persuasiveness.

—*Sir Arthur Thomas Quiller-Couch*

During my senior year of college in 1987 I signed up for an independent study course in China–U.S. diplomatic history of the 1950s. I wanted to read the complete works of the writers whose books individually I loved—John Paton Davies Jr., John Stewart Service, Barbara Tuchman, Edgar Snow, and George F. Kennan, among others—all together in a concentrated program of study. My supervisor and I got along very well, and every week we discussed my selections both formally and informally. At one meeting I told him that since my teens I had found Barbara Tuchman and George Kennan easy to agree with.

He replied with a smile that they were both great writers, and that it was easy for readers to let the quality of their writing seduce them into agreeing with their arguments. The professor spoke as one who himself had been "seduced" more than once. I agreed with him, but that exchange was one of the first times I had seriously thought about the medium having so much influence that it might actually override the message and assume its own distinct form. Yes, I had read Marshall McLuhan's and Quentin Fiore's *The Medium is the Massage*,[1] and I had been a public speaker for several years, but as yet I had not recognized that truly great writing is itself propaganda.

THE STRUCTURE OF A PERSUASIVE ESSAY

As mentioned in the Preface, persuasive writing relies principally on argument to influence readers to adopt or understand a particular viewpoint.

Persuasion is used in every subject when the author needs to convince his or her readers of opinions or facts. Students, businesspeople, diplomats, politicians, teachers, poets, advertising executives, and novelists use persuasive writing. Whenever readers need to be convinced about a situation or viewpoint, and the author has the facts, quotations, and structure to construct a reasonable essay or article, he or she develops persuasive writing.

There are different types of persuasive writing. The five-paragraph essay usually focuses on one topic and the author develops her or his argument from a statement of fact or opinion through paragraphs that support the topic. The final paragraph often is a restatement of the original paragraph, which has been strengthened by the previous fact-filled paragraphs.

A longer essay, article, or sermon may be structured similarly, but usually incorporates more topics, opinions, and arguments. A persuasive book, such as this one, may divide topics into chapters and provide several subjects or examples in each chapter to cover a subject more thoroughly.

Advertisers try to persuade consumers to buy their products by presenting the qualities that will influence the public. A product may be marketed to make a person or place safer, or cleaner, or to promote wealth, happiness, ease, flavor—the list is large, but the message is that the person will be better off with the product.

It is important to know how to write persuasively because we humans frequently have to explain ourselves. Writing well to persuade is a valuable tool, whether we seek good grades, a job or a promotion, or, in a larger context, a change in how we think or live. Persuasive writing is an important building block of society; it can be used to create—or destroy—almost anything.

A persuasive argument may begin with an author's point of view, "Our community is facing a tragic loss"; or a list of facts about a premise or situation, "The library's first, second, and third folios may be sold to raise money, because the library cannot pay its bills"; or a combination of facts and the author's perspective, "If the library's first, second, and third folios were to be sold to raise money, the community would lose." The author may then incorporate any or all of the tools of factual evidence, logic, and a challenge to the audience to act.

The following excerpts from *Essay Start* set out a model of a persuasive essay that this book expands upon and provides examples of. *Essay Start* provides wonderful descriptions and examples of many types of essays. Its home page for a persuasive essay, which contains links to other relevant pages and a sample essay, is listed in the notes for this chapter. Included in its advice are these important points:

Note: Do not confuse facts with truths. A "truth" is an idea believed by many people, but it cannot be proven.

Statistics—These can provide excellent support. Be sure your statistics come from responsible sources. Always cite your sources.

Quotes—Direct quotes from leading experts that support your position are invaluable.

Examples—Examples enhance your meaning and make your ideas concrete. They are the proof. Be well informed about your topic.[2]

Following is a recommendation of how to structure a five-paragraph persuasive essay.[3]

1. A statement of a position, a fact, or an action.
2. Information to explain and back up one of the points in the statement.
3. Information to explain and back up another of the points in the statement.
4. Information to explain and back a third point in the statement.
5. A conclusion or summary drawn from the previous points.

For specific information on transitions between sentences and paragraphs, see the "Transitional Words and Phrases" section later in this chapter.

The conclusion of a persuasive essay should restate the writer's position using the facts that have already been presented. A good summary of the main points concludes a five-paragraph persuasive essay.

The strategies for presenting perspectives change through the years. These days, a conversational tone in writing and speaking is fashionable. Writers and presenters are often encouraged to have a conversation with their audience, be it in writing or speech. As I write this, Barack Obama is having a conversation with the convention delegates who have nominated him as the party's choice for president; closer to home, a pending refresher workshop about the Americans with Disabilities Act as it relates to libraries is thought to be structured more effectively as a conversation with the participant librarians. These conversations can be effective media, but can they work in exclusively written formats as well as spoken?

THE ENTICEMENT

The enticement of writing to persuade an audience of a point, a subject, perhaps a new way of thought! You know basically (or in detail) what you want to say and basically (or in detail) who your readership is—there is more detail about those topics later in this chapter. Now you are pondering a structure to use to present your magnum opus, or great work. The world of writing offers many formats for persuasion; persuasiveness is pervasive. Forms of persuasion vary. There is the threat, "Don't be foolish—your compatriot has already confessed." There is the less terrifying statement that is also flavored with threat: "Please pledge to your Public Broadcasting Station now, so that we may continue to bring you these wonderful programs." There is the personal, "He will never look away when you are wearing lingerie by Herman's." There are more subtle approaches, such as the team spirit one: "We could provide a greater variety of programs if our budget were increased by 10 percent, so it's up to all of you to make a difference." There is the positive change approach: "I ordered my lingerie from Herman's; now I am married to a billionaire and run my own small country."

The carrot-and-stick approach is familiar to most parents: "If you eat your vegetables, then you can have dessert." Then there is one used by editors of some publishing houses, which is, everyone hopes, frequently effective: "If you send in the completed manuscript by the deadline, we will be able to publish it sooner, and we will have an opinion of you as an author who honors contracts." These are fairly decent propositions, and if bribery is involved, well, that is not an unusual aspect of persuasion.

One form that can be of great value is a personal or professional assessment. It is highly persuasive when based on the true feelings of the one who is assessing herself. A few months ago a clergyperson and I were having a heart-to-heart talk about many issues, including ministers' roles and responsibilities. She said a minister's job is to offer hope. It was a statement I agreed with, first, because I had always thought it, too, and it is easy for me to agree with someone whose thoughts are compatible with mine. Another significant point was that for that particular minister, as well as others, hope is the basic function of ministry: something she and her colleagues are called upon to offer and can offer consistently—there is hope, even when there may be little else.

So far we have looked at aspects of logic, propaganda, fear, bribery, and truth as components of persuasion. They all mingle with facts in a persuasive essay, so that the readers or listeners get an acceptable mixture of thoughts and feelings working to convince them of the writers' or speakers' perspectives. Look at the essay "My Experiences during the Peace Corps Clearance Process" to assess what its message is, how the facts and emotions are presented, and if the essay is effective. I wrote the report for a presentation that documents part of the process of my becoming a Peace Corps volunteer, a process that required significant persuasion.

MY EXPERIENCES DURING THE PEACE CORPS CLEARANCE PROCESS

The Peace Corps' medical department was as reluctant to pass me as it was to say exactly why it was reluctant to pass me. For many months all that the nurse practitioners would say was that my application was "under consideration," although by some amazingly repetitive process the same test and its replacements managed to fall out of my folder two or three times and apparently no one noticed. The deadline for Morocco had passed and it was thought that I might be re-routed, but first I had to obtain medical clearance. The medical assessments are done by nurse practitioners based on forms that are filled out by the recruit's own medical practitioner. The Americans with Disabilities Act was relatively new, having been passed in 1990 to be in force in 1992, and admitting disabled people to the Peace Corps was a relatively new process of which its medical department was evidently fearful. What angered me about the medical department was the nurses' apparent stonewalling, since I offered many times to answer any questions they had concerning my disability. Finally, the Boston Regional Office advised me to call the regional director about the situation. After speaking to her about it I said essentially, "I truly don't mean this as a threat, but if this [stonewalling] is happening in my case, it's happening in others. A few years from now, if the situation with medical is not addressed, the Peace Corps may find itself in the same situation re: disabled people as the Foreign Service was with the women." A few years before, Foreign Service officers and former candidates had filed a successful class-action suit against the Foreign Service for gender bias and discrimination.

"You're absolutely right," she agreed, and after a few more sentences—she was cordial and responsive throughout the telephone call—we hung up. Within a few days I received my medical clearance and a letter of apology from the Peace Corps nurse practitioners.

After my graduation in June of that year, I continued to work at Simmons College until the autumn, and then began work at the Providence Athenaeum in January, while the person in charge of my file tried to find another country for which I was medically cleared. There had been some legitimate restrictions to my medical clearance. During one telephone call, she asked if I might be willing to wait another year, when they might be more certain of placing me. I demurred, reminding her that I had been nominated in December 1995, it was now 1997, and although I hoped that it worked out for that year I really didn't want to put my life on hold for yet another year. She expressed sympathy and understanding, and after 19 months of negotiation, I was offered a place in training on June 10, 1997, as a (as it was then called) youth at risk volunteer in Jamaica.

During its first 10 years Peace Corps training was based on that of the paramilitary and geared to young people who were in top physical condition. In the early 1970s, the training became more culture and language based rather than physically intensive and the way was opened for people of different ages and certain physical challenges to join. In my group were some people of retirement age, and one woman who had a significant hearing impairment who lip-read with remarkable facility.

Other tools of persuasion can be very effective. There is the use of irony, such as this example, courtesy of Frank B. Gilbreth Jr., in *Time Out for Happiness*, of an experience his parents shared after a serious illness survived by motion study expert Frank Sr. in 1917 (The language, from 1917, is other than politically correct):

> Frank said devoutly, "*anything* is better than being in the Fort Sill Hospital. I'd rather be [seriously disabled] on the outside than be in that hell-hole with only a hangnail."
> "Exactly," nodded [Frank, Sr.'s business partner and wife] Lillie. "So you see how lucky you are?"
> "I'm just a lucky duck," said Frank, still a mite bitterly. . . . "Sure, I'm so stiff I can hardly move, my joints are swollen, and a fat man—well, anyway, pleasingly plump—and crutches don't mix. But I'm a lucky duck."
> "And so am I," smiled Lillie, "to have such a brave and cheerful husband who . . ."
> "A lucky duck," repeated Frank, with a little less sarcasm.[4]

There are many uses of humor to clarify points, such as the kind President Franklin Delano Roosevelt used on numerous occasions. For example, "Now I don't mind attacks . . . and my family doesn't mind attacks . . . but Fala [his terrier], *does*."[5] The basic structure of persuasive writing follows the form of many or all of these: introduction, examples, reasons/arguments, counterarguments, and conclusion(s).

Here is an example of a discussion of the development of a high school project. I received this message from a friend who was student teaching in a high school in Illinois and figuring out how to make a class project on the Puritans come to life.

> I love the time [period], but the readings can be a little dry. I have to fig-
> ure out how to juice it up a little. I have no fear about the Salem Witch
> Trials[.][6]

My reply:

> Something to begin, I think, is to impress upon the students that crossing
> the Atlantic in the 1600s was considerably more hazardous than going to
> the moon was in the 1960s (and received much, much less sympathetic PR,
> since the people who left were rebelling against the Crown, and treason usu-
> ally meant death, and they were given permission to go in part to promote
> the colonization process that had begun in the 15th century with you-know-
> who). The people who took the risk had to be tremendously motivated to
> do so. I'd suggest discussing that motivation beyond what is described dryly
> in the literature. What is it like truly to feel every day that you may not sur-
> vive, and that your sole security is trust in a Higher Power? (I don't know if,
> these days, you can mention God in public school, but the Puritans' faith
> was all-important to them.)[7]

In my message, the moon is used as a counterexample to the Puritans' crossing the Atlantic. The background and the hazards they faced are reasons, and their ultimate decision to attempt the crossing and put their faith in a Higher Power is the conclusion.

In *Writing History: A Guide for Students*, William Kelleher Storey advises,

> Writers must give their readers reasons to care. Many historians use the be-
> ginning of an essay or book to connect their scholarly interests to broader
> academic and political debates. For example, . . . [historian] Caroline Walker
> Bynum . . . grabs the reader's attention:[8]
>
> Sex and money . . . again and again modern scholars have emphasized the
> guilt engendered by their seductiveness, the awesome heroism required for
> their renunciation. Yet this modern focus may tell us more about the twenti-
> eth century than about the late Middle Ages. In our industrialized corner of
> the globe, where food supplies do not fail, we scarcely notice grain or milk,
> ever-present supports of life, and yearn rather after money or sexual favors
> as signs of power or of success.[9]

Storey's lesson is that a well-constructed and moderate argument that is presented by citing authoritative sources is effective and can influence even those who may disagree with it. You can sustain your readers' or listeners' interest by making the essay personal, or through the use of contemporary comparisons. At times, particularly if you have been asked to write or present something because of your personal experience or expertise, it is appropriate to include your own interests and perspectives, while incorporating the larger issues of your topic in your essay. Storey was focusing on historical essays, but the advice is valid for any persuasive essay. He advised addressing the questions, "What are the broader . . . problems that your essay addresses?" "Why have you chosen your specific topic to explore these interests?" "What argument will be developing over the course of your essay?"[10]

THE PRESENTATION

Presentations differ from essays and articles because they are delivered orally—from notes or from fully written texts—and because the speaker's body language and use of voice and expressions become part of the process. What you know and feel about your subject will be even more apparent to an audience during a presentation than during the reading of an essay or article. A presentation allows additional scope to persuade by the effective use of the face, voice, and body combined. The presenter's appearance and method of delivery—which includes self-confidence, cleanliness, neatness, posture, vocal quality, and the establishment of a relationship with the audience—become extremely significant. These are significant components of the difference between an essay, which can be written in pajamas and with wet hair, and a personal appearance.

Josh Gordon, the author of *Presentations That Change Minds: Strategies to Persuade, Convince and Get Results,* lists, in descending order, common practices presenters use: sharing facts, offering solutions, sharing ideas, storytelling, and ultimately, changing audiences' perceptions.[11] Among the strategies Gordon recommends are those that "deeply involved" the audience by inviting, even commanding, their curiosity and participation.[12]

Establishing connections between the speaker and the audience is a common method of generating involvement. What can the speaker present in a package of experiences that interests a particular audience? Generally, human interest is most effective when you know your audience, and audiences' reactions can add tremendously to the presentations. I was pleasantly surprised and entertained during one of my presentations when, in response to a vignette I told about Senator Robert Dole's being transported to his home in a body cast for surgery after being injured during World War II, several audience members from "the best generation," responded with their own stories and stories of their friends who were veterans. We enjoyed about five minutes of reminiscences in which I was an enthusiastically active listener. I couldn't make a firsthand contribution to those anecdotes because I was born 15 years after the end of that war.

A presentation I gave on the topic of the inclusion of students with disabilities in public school classrooms sparked an impromptu discussion among a roomful of teacher candidates about their thoughts and apprehensions. The discussion relaxed the audience, and the listeners became more receptive more quickly to my talk than they would have had I been the only one sharing information. The presenter learns a fantastic amount of information in presentations geared to audience involvement, and the audience helps to shape the presentation, so that it receives and responds to the perspectives presented with significantly more energy and interest than it would were its members passive listeners. Similar audience participation evolved from a workshop on mediation during role-playing exercises, and at a show-and-tell presentation in which the audience members were successively blindfolded and loosely tied up to simulate disabling conditions, then given opportunities to move around in their different states. The participants then reported to the rest of the audience on the ways in which they adjusted to being temporarily disabled—how they felt, how they processed what senses and movements they could use, and how they proceeded to use their newly altered perceptions and skills.

A speaker can structure most presentations to include audience participation, although the planning may be more challenging because it requires the speaker's scheduling exercises for the audience—for example, a "What Would You Do in This Case?" participation, question, and answer session, or just time for input from the listeners, as well as the ability to let go of some control of the presentation.

Introduction to Establish the Writer's Legitimacy
Power Relationships

The word "author" is derived from the word "authority," and it defines intellectual creation. People who write for an audience other than themselves are assuming or have been given authority on a topic. The audience, however, has a significant role in the relationship, as it is not only receiving but evaluating the message—and frequently, by extension, the author. How an author indicates his legitimacy to write about a particular theme, subject, or format is a situation familiar to anyone who has written an article or book proposal. Authors present their credentials as what they have done, how they have been educated, and the amount of time they have spent in the field or researching the topic. When presenting credentials, you may also want to mention with whom you've worked or studied and, when presenting the subject, what chief sources you used as references.

The Audience as Judge (and Sometimes Jury and Executioner!)

Your readership is very important. A well-informed audience will evaluate your content. At times, your audience will assess the content not only for its own edification but also for the author's academic or professional advancement. The authority to influence the author, then, is in the hands of the audience.

You must think of the expectations of an audience and focus on ways to satisfy them. You need to present yourself as qualified to present your material, that is, worthy of the time that the readership gives you.

Some Examples of Establishing Authority for an Audience

The following examples illustrate a way of establishing legitimacy as an author. The first example is an extended curriculum vitae that describes my mediation and library science education and professional experience:

CURRICULUM VITAE INFORMATION

I have worked in Northern Ireland as an intern in mediation, in Turkey as a delegate to a peace conference, in Jamaica as a Peace Corps volunteer, in Wales as a researcher and an adviser to undergraduates at the University of Wales, Cardiff, and, relevant to all of this, as an assistant to the Warburg Professor of International Relations and later, consultant and conference coordinator to the Simmons College Office of Student Life regarding issues of the Americans with Disabilities Act of 1990 and the older Section 504.

After obtaining a library degree and working first, while a library science student, as a researcher for the Warburg Professor of International Relations at Simmons College, and then after graduation as an Internet Reference Librarian at the Providence Athenaeum in Rhode Island, I joined the Peace Corps in 1997. I was in the Youth at Risk sector, as it was then called, in Kingston, Jamaica, and was assigned first to Abilities Foundation, a vocational school for young adults that had been the brainchild of an earlier Peace Corps volunteer, then transferred to the Jamaica Council for Persons with Disabilities, run by Ransford Wright. In the capacities of librarian and researcher I conducted a national survey that led to the development of the Jamaica Coalition on Disability. That work encompassed public speaking also. They were truly surprised at my stopping the chair to insist, in what I've come to recognize as my "superpower voice"—that is, two parts the late Katharine Hepburn and one part the late Franklin Roosevelt—"Let's find an alternate route." As I say, this tone surprises some, but on more than one occasion it has prevented my becoming the late Carolyn Davis.[13]

The preceding and following passages are samples from a speech I presented to the International Women's Club in Providence, Rhode Island. They illustrate the development of background, authority, and experience to build to points of audience conversion.

When on behalf of Ellie and you, Maxine invited me to speak to you about my experiences as a person who is disabled who has worked in other countries, I realized that this presented my first opportunity to tell some of "my story behind the story," and I began rubbing my hands in anticipation.

These next sections outline and explain some of my professional life and its development. Explanations are key in a persuasive essay or article, because explanations enable the audience not only to understand the situations but also the background and how the situations evolved.

From mediation to library science:

In late 1992 and early 1993 I worked first as an intern in conflict management in Coleraine, Northern Ireland, then as an independent researcher in Stroke City, so-called because whether it was known by the designated name "Londonderry," or "Derry," depended on the Protestant or Catholic affiliation of the speaker.

After that difficult time, I decided to change from conflict to generic research. A practical way to make the change was to get a master's degree in library science. I looked at a few places that offered the program: the University of North Carolina at Chapel Hill, the University of Rhode Island, and the Graduate School of Library and Information Science at Simmons College in Boston. As I recall, I applied to the programs at the University of Rhode Island and Simmons, citing access and my desire to work part-time as a particular need and interest, respectively. To my surprise, Simmons sent me many letters of detail regarding physical access and encouragement to attend. As a small private college, it had the staff and means to do this.[14]

Simmons ultimately persuaded me to attend, as all graduate schools must that compete for students, by addressing the prospective student's needs, in this case my need for part-time work and physical access. I received several letters assuring me of the many employment options that Simmons offered, as well as the ease of access of the campus.

> Deciding on Simmons, I moved into a dormitory (at age 34) and prepared yet again to be "Dorm Mom," the oldest one in the building. To my surprise and gratification I wasn't; a man in his late fifties was in the apartment across the hall.
>
> He was a retired Foreign Service officer who had been ambassador to Somalia and Rwanda some years previous. During one of our early meetings I told him a little bit of my international relations background, while musing to myself about the irony of beginning a library course to qualify as a "generic" researcher, only to have an international relations specialist as my neighbor.[15]

The former ambassador and I had a sort of reverse job interview. He asked me if I would be interested in conducting research for him, and I replied that although I had conducted international relations research in the past, now I was interested in conducting more generic research. He responded by telling me what his research needs from me were.

> I became his research assistant and we began planning seminars, an average of one per month, for which invited guests who were specialists concerning or VIPs of particular countries or areas spoke and answered questions for approximately 90 minutes. Among the guests were diplomats and academics, of course, but also high-profile public-relations people, such as the president of Ireland.

PEACE CORPS, JAMAICA

One meeting the professor arranged for his undergraduate students featured a recruiter from the Boston Peace Corps office and had an audience of three or four, including the Warburg Professor and me. The woman presented the complete recruitment program and laughed as she said that in the past she had presented to an audience of as "few" as one. Within a week I called the local office.

The standard Peace Corps process for clearance and placement takes from 9 to 18 months. The candidates are age 21 years or older, and the stages of the application process cover the following:

1. An interview with and subsequent nomination by a local recruitment officer. This may be done by telephone if the prospective candidate lives a considerable distance from a recruitment office.
2. FBI clearance.
3. Medical clearance by that particular Peace Corps department.

4. An invitation by the Peace Corps to join a particular group and country: for example, Group 68, Jamaica.
5. The candidate's acceptance, followed by the issuance of a Peace Corps passport. The Americans with Disabilities Act has made acceptance of people with disabilities easier, but a candidate's assertiveness and knowledge of the law are assets and were necessities in my own case.[16]

Now the essay shifts from one type of work, research that results in a concrete result, to more theoretical research in a different country. The aspects of a persuasive essay that are used are background, description, points of view, and a conclusion.

WALES (2001–2006)

I went to Wales primarily to gather information about the relationships between the Principality of Wales and England in the 14th century, learn Welsh, and discern if particular conflict theories developed in the 20th century apply to certain situations and structures of the medieval period. On a previous trip, I had been asked to write an article for the journal *Technicalities* about an international graduate summer school in library technology. When I returned I was asked by the editor, Sheila Intner, to continue with a series to be called, "Tales from Wales."[17]

I learned a lot about Cardiff's academic system during that time, and what I experienced was staggering. In America, a research candidate chooses his or her dissertation committee. In Wales, people were assigned to assess my thesis who had no knowledge of one of the subjects, and they admitted it. Britain and America invert the terms, "thesis" and "dissertation." In Britain, a long research project is a thesis. In America, it is a dissertation, which is what shorter academic final papers are called in Britain.

A positive aspect of the experience was that I made a good friend who was one of the leaders of the Women's Archive of Wales, which is essentially a bunch of collections in towns and cities throughout Wales. The collections range from historical documents and photographs to memorabilia, which were often identified and sometimes collected through roadshows. The roadshow settings, to which different members of the group travel to different locations, are patterned after PBS's *Antiques Roadshow*. People like them.

Another plus was that "Tales from Wales" was well received. Librarians who read it sent me e-mail messages. I enjoyed a medium-term correspondence with one person.

Wales was a mixture of experiences for me. It was truly educational, although not always sensible.

Persuading to Convert

Points of view can be developed into reasoned arguments and stories to sway readers into a particular perspective that they may not have considered. Persuasive arguments are used in instruction to demonstrate to readers why particular methods are preferable to others. An example below is from *A Manual for Writers of Research Papers, Theses, and Dissertations*, by Kate L. Turabian.

> Some writers think that once they have an outline or storyboard, they can draft by just grinding out sentences. If you've written a lot to explore your ideas, you may even think that you can plug that preliminary writing into a draft. Experienced writers know better. They know two things: exploratory writing is crucial but often not right for a draft, and thoughtful drafting can be an act of discovery that planning and storyboarding can prepare them for, but never replace. In fact, most writers don't know what they *can* think until they see it appear in words before them. Indeed, you experience one of the most exciting moments in research when you discover yourself expressing ideas that you didn't know you had until that moment.[18]

As illustrated in the Turabian example, persuasive arguments, like characters in a book, may take on lives of their own as they are written. The process of developing a persuasive argument is more than just gathering data and presenting a point of view. By Turabian's example, it becomes an evolving mental exercise that can be outside an author's premeditated control. Persuasive writing becomes an outlet for the author's developing consciousness.

Appendix 21a from *Why We Must Run with Scissors*, by Barry Lane and Gretchen Bernabei, illustrates "Persuasive Moments as Poems: *The Odyssey*" in different formats written by school-age persuaders. The poems, "Recipe for a Good Hero," "The Sailor's Speech to his Comrades, Just Before Opening His Bag of Wind," and "Calypso Begs Odysseus"[19] use examples of kindliness, humor, anger, hunger, suspicion, love, and sex as powerful tools of persuasion.

The writing process creates its own emotions, which can vary from desolation to euphoria, but the task must be completed. Nearly all of the chapters in this guide offer practical suggestions and examples to deal with time pressure, structural problems, and writer's block. In a persuasive essay entitled,

"The Answer to Stress," the 15-year-old author describes a few examples of stress-producing incidents, then, using documented facts in addition to his own persuasiveness, illustrates and describes physical and psychological reasons why comfort food is beneficial to eat in those and any other stress-producing circumstance. The combination of his good writing and documented evidence persuades readers to consider his argument—this essay persuaded me to indulge my passion more often for fried chicken, especially when I am facing a deadline.[20]

This type of writing can be applied to any persuasive essay for high school. The structure would be valid for many other forms and levels of persuasive writing for university and graduate-school essays, as well those at professional levels.

For an example of a persuasive essay about a professional experience, following is an excerpt that describes a process of integration and persuasion during the installation of PCs for Internet use in the Providence Athenaeum. This article documents a persuasive course of action in a historic library.

WAS THIS CHANGE HANDLED WELL VIS À VIS THE LIBRARY DIRECTOR AND PATRONS?

I believe that the Director handled that particular transition appropriately.

1. He identified and responded to the demand by presenting it to the Providence Athenaeum's Board of Trustees as a project that required initiation, then with the Board's knowledge hired staff, identified and applied for funding to set up the networking.
2. The Director and staff sought to assure the patrons by addressing their concerns directly in the context of the Athenaeum's progressive history, and its need to remain not only progressive, but competitive in the present and future for its continued existence. This line of reason was developed in such a way that it encouraged the inclusion of all the patrons and at the time won over all but the diehards.[21]

Additionally, no one was coerced into learning the new system, or made to feel that her position was at risk. Neither the technology nor the library's new policy was a threat to anyone's job. The transition was successful because the director and assistant director followed an inclusive, easy course during the transition, during which a necessary part of modernization was introduced and integrated into the existing environment without hurting anyone. Thoughtfulness and planning can lead to success for everyone, and painless, all-inclusive success is a marvelous persuader.

To change the subject, a child receives a significant lesson in life when she first sees a parent as a human being. Following is an example of a mother and daughter bonding in a different way through a shared experience. Its persuasiveness is in its descriptions of the experience.

HAPPY AT HOME WITH PNEUMONIA

February 1969 stays in my mind as one of the happiest times of my childhood. I had a chest cold that developed in its second week into pneumonia, thus allowing my mother and me some truly relaxing, homebound experiences together, coupled with a feeling of fugitives at rest and play while those of the rest of our world worked. My mother and I lived together by ourselves most of the time, since my siblings were both at college and my parents were divorced. At nine, I had something of a lock-step, rigid schedule of school, nearly annual surgery, and physical therapy for cerebral palsy, and my mother's schedule was the more so, as she was obliged to teach junior high school, keep our home, and direct my therapy regimen.

Ah, then, a week of enforced rest was a welcome relief for both of us. I remember only two clouds to mar our holiday: my persistent cough and the ever-looming grape cough medicine that had to be taken every four hours. I actually liked my antibiotics that were in tablet form, but the cough medicine tasted and reacted in my stomach bad enough to remind me that I was sick.

I don't think I had ever seen my mother at play much before, except on weekends, but she certainly was that week. Beginning late in the morning after breakfast and continuing after my afternoon nap, we played countless games of Scrabble. She usually won them, but I pleased myself no end by drawing my first Triple Word Score, and a nine-letter word that I regret to say I've forgotten. The second day, my mother drew out the Scrabble board with an apologetic giggle and, "Would you like to play some more?" to which I agreed, very happy to be playing with her. I was fueled during the word games by cups of tea, ostensibly to loosen the congestion, but actually, I believe, as a bribe to play, for tea was my favorite beverage and it occurred rarely in my life in those days. I wouldn't have required a bribe, however, because it was such a treat to do something with my mother that was fun and out-of-schedule.

During my nap and again at night, my mother indulged her favorite hobbies: solving crossword puzzles and reading mystery books. How she delighted in the works of Erle Stanley Gardiner, Agatha Christie, Ngaio Marsh, and others—so much so that she read chapters to me in order not to break the flow. I encouraged her by making editorial comments:

"Della Street works a lot. . . . Suppose the defendant's guilty, what would Perry Mason do? . . . Why can't they tell that someone is going to die because the detective's there?" I would have been wary of inviting Hercule Poirot or Jane Marple to *our* house, and it seemed strange that all of those owners of the manors and estates where Poirot's or Marple's acquaintances routinely were murdered didn't feel the same way. Someone died of pneumonia in one of the stories, and while I laughed myself into more coughing, my mother amended softly that, "Those were the days before penicillin," then began to laugh too.

I think what was special about that week was my beginning to be acquainted with the fun-loving, laughter-driven side of my mother, a side of her that as a child I rarely saw, but from that time looked to see with increasing frequency, particularly during vacations. For a few years I'd hoped that we might have a repeat of that week sometime, however, I remained healthy. We played a lot of Scrabble from then on, but I missed the stolen moments feeling of that February.

A challenge to you, now. If you were writing a similar story, how might you structure it?

TRANSITIONAL WORDS AND PHRASES

As authors develop their arguments, the effective use of transitional phrases is crucial.[22] Transitional words and phrases introduce material, time and place relationships, and changes in those relationships. Writers and speakers use transitional phrases so much, however, that it can be easy to forget their specific strategic uses. Transitional phrases enable writers to drive through their various points and pit stops.

Some transitional words and phrases demonstrate additions, for example "again," "and," "as well as," "as a result," "besides," "both," and "consequently." Others suggest a numbered order, for example "one," "two," "first," "second," "then," "too," and "also." In short, a transitional word or phrase is anything that introducing an additional phrase, word, or meaning to a sentence.[23]

Words that demonstrate contrast include "but," "on the contrary," "in spite of," "conversely," and "at the same time." Contrast indicates a comparison. Concession phrases that indicate the acknowledgment or yielding of a point include "although," "at least," "conceding that," and "still."[24]

"Detail" words can be used for written transitions, too. Besides "in detail," other such words and phrases include "specifically," "especially," "to explain," and "including." Suggestions are also a type of transition, such as "with this in mind," and "therefore."[25]

Examples of Transitional Words in Essays

Following is an excerpt from a persuasive essay entitled, "A Research Slice of Life":

> The treatments and understanding of the human body in the 1960s were fairly primitive by twenty-first century standards, to a considerable degree because technology had not advanced enough to enable people to observe as much of the function of living bodies as they do today. However, attitudes regarding the practice of rehabilitative treatments were changing. Particularly notable to me in the early seventies was the vast improvement in 1970s New York from 1960s Rhode Island. That was a prerequisite for the tidal wave of information, new treatments, patient participation, and the multitude of possibilities that were to manifest during the next thirty years and beyond.[26]

Notice the use of the words "however," "particularly notable," and "prerequisite for a tidal wave of information." They signal that significant points are about to be made. Transitional words and phrases are important in persuasive writing and speaking because the author carries the readers or audience from one way of thought to another, which requires the reader or audience to make an adjustment in thought.

FIGURES OF SPEECH

Tropes and Schemes

Trope: The use of words or phrases in an unusual way. One example is "He's so ugly that he's cute."

Scheme: Words used in an unusual order. One example, "A waist is a terrible thing to mind." My friend Maxine of the International Women's Club, who is giving this text the benefit of her professional editor's experience, reminds me that "the word 'waste' also became 'waist,' a lesson in homonyms!"[27]

Tropes and schemes are tools used in "[r]hetoric, 'the art of effective speaking.'"[28] The main rhetorical topics are definition, comparison, relationship, circumstance, and testimony. Definition is broken down "by genus [type]" and "[b]y division" and is used to define a topic minutely—in legal arguments, for example.[29] Comparison encompasses "similarity and difference . . . as well as 'degree',"[30] or the proportion of things that can be compared. Relationship is defined by the categories of cause and effect, antecedent and consequence, or the events that lead to the conclusion, a logical argument. Relationship also includes contraries, which are the degrees of potential truth or falsehood between similar things. Another category of relationship, contradictions, allows for no degrees or quibbling in comparison: when one situation is true, the other is false.[31] The topic circumstance is broken down into "[t]he possible and the impossible," basically, pairs of contraries or similarities of which both must be either possible or impossible.[32] Examples of possible discourses are "If you can imprison a man, you can make him mayor," or "If a person can learn trigonometry, she can learn algebra." The last topic is testimony, which can be defined broadly in the subcategories of authority, testimonial, statistics, maxims, law, and precedent.[33] None of the subcategories of testimony is unshakable in terms of truth or absolutes; I think of their similarity only as originating outside the speaker's experience, so, even if a precedent has been set or a maxim created by the speaker, the speaker is obliged to cite another source or quote someone.

Rewording Phrases

The following is an example of guiding the readers to a different viewpoint. It is an excerpt of a summary of mine for a yet-to-be-written speech, of something that appears to be a daunting subject—power relationships between the English and Welsh administrations of the 14th-century Principality of Wales.

This manuscript demonstrates the interrelationships, particularly in power structures, between the key actors of Crown administration in England with the key actors of the principality, particularly those influenced by the Crown administration, beginning with Prince Llywelyn the Last to the leader of the rebellion of the early 15th century, Owain Glyndŵr, and some key players in between. Examples of crisis times are also provided, including the epidemics of plague in the mid-14th century and the rebellion and insurrections of Rhys ap Maredudd, Madog ap Llywelyn, and the displaced nobleman Owain ap [son of] Thomas ap [son of] Rhodri, who at least temporarily had the backing of the king of France, thus making his claim to regain his lands an international issue. Infused in part by these actions and helped along by the bards, poets, and other discontented elites, the Glyndŵr Rebellion ushered in the 15th century, which led to the Punitive Acts of 1401–1402 and a restriction against claims for "Injuries Sustained in the Late Rebellion"[34] in 1413. The principality might have been completely crushed, particularly after the Glyndŵr

Rebellion, but it survived and developed into the beginning of a modern nation to continue its uneasy process of coexistence and synthesis.[35] By 1415, population distribution, settlement patterns, forms of agriculture, networks of towns, lines of trade, and the distribution of wealth and power had changed significantly in the principalities of North and South Wales. The Crown's Welsh possessions had changed from their 11th-century medieval models closer to their 17th-century early modern ones.[36]

Occasional summaries and the very occasional rewording of a phrase or passage to make its meaning clearer in the text or presentation can provide welcome relief, as in these examples:

On the whole, I mean, I couldn't say absolutely, but my feeling is inclined to be negative.
So you won't do it?
No.

To reference persuasive George Kennan, here is a summary of a controversy that he ignited. The State Department published this on one of its Web pages and included a few additional explanations. The bracketed explanation is mine.

[George Kennan's State Department colleague] Nitze, who saw the Soviet threat primarily in military terms, interpreted Kennan's call for "the adroit and vigilant application of counter-force" to mean the use of military power. In contrast, Kennan, who considered the Soviet threat to be primarily political, advocated above all else economic assistance (e.g., the Marshall Plan) and "psychological warfare" (overt propaganda and covert operations) to counter the spread of Soviet influence. In 1950, Nitze's conception of containment won out over Kennan's. NSC 68, a policy document prepared by the National Security Council and signed by Truman, called for a drastic expansion of the U.S. military budget. The paper also expanded containment's scope beyond the defense of major centers of industrial power to encompass the entire world. "In the context of the present polarization of power," it read, "a defeat of free institutions anywhere is a defeat everywhere."[37]

The essay concludes with a brief, general summary of subsequent Cold War policies:

Despite all the criticisms and the various policy defeats that Kennan suffered in the early 1950's, containment in the more general sense of blocking the expansion of Soviet influence remained the basic strategy of the United States throughout the cold war. On the one hand, the United States did not withdraw into isolationism; on the other, it did not move to "roll back" Soviet power, as John Foster Dulles briefly advocated. It is possible to say that each succeeding administration after Truman's, until the collapse of communism in 1989, adopted a variation of Kennan's containment policy and made it their own.[38]

In this example, a few parenthetical explanations and a summary can keep the audience involved and interested. The use of restatement and explanations, as well as a general summary, is especially helpful when the audience does not have the same familiarity with the topic as a speaker or author, and the person's job is to instruct and persuade. Be careful about restatements, though. Use them sparingly or your audience or readers may think you are patronizing or writing down to them. The subsequent chapters contain much more about appropriate paths to take to show your audience how you are reasoning, what you are feeling, and how to present topics.

Well-informed and structured persuasive writing and presentations are true arts, and when done well, are enlightening, entertaining, and influential.

NOTES

"*Quotes*" Sir Arthur Quiller-Couch, "Persuasiveness," www.yourdictionary.com/quotes/persuasiveness

1. Marshall McLuhan and Quentin Fiore, *The Medium Is the Massage* (Corte Madera, CA: Gingko Press, 1967).

2. *Essay Start: Your Guide to Better Essays*, "Types of Essays: PersuasiveEssays," www.essaystart.com/Kinds_of Essays/persuasiv_Essays.htm.

3. *Persuasive Writing, 9th Grade English*, my.uen.org/mydocuments/downloadfile?userid=jlafortune&documentid=6177354 Alt. grammar.ccc.commnet.edu/grammar/five_par.htm.

4. Frank B. Gilbreth Jr., *Time Out for Happiness* (New York: Thomas Y. Crowell Company, 1970), 163.

5. EIR Online, Online Almanac, From Volume 4, Issue Number 38 of *EIR Online*, (September 20, 2005), 16. www.larouchepub.com/eiw/public/2005/2005_30-39/2005_30-39/2005-38/pdf/alltxtv4n38.pdf.

6. Kim Shafer, e-mail message to Carolyn Davis (September 13, 2008).

7. Carolyn Davis, e-mail message to Kim Shafer (September 13, 2008).

8. William Kelleher Storey, *Writing History: A Guide for Students*, 7th ed. (New York: Oxford University Press, 2004), 68.

9. Caroline Walker Bynum, *Holy Feast and Holy Fast: The Religious Significance of Food to Medieval Women* (Berkeley: University of California Press, 1987), 1. Quoted in *Writing History: A Guide for Students*, 68.

10. Storey, *Writing History*, 68–69.

11. Heath Row, "Persuasive Presentations," *Fast Company*, www.fastcompany.com/blog/heath-row/persuasive-presentations.

12. Josh Gordon, *Presentations That Change Minds: Strategies to Persuade, Convince and Get Results* (New York: McGraw-Hill, 2006), 5.

13. Carolyn Davis, "My Career in International Research," presentation to the International Women's Club, Providence, RI (November 26, 2008).

14. Ibid.

15. Ibid.

16. Ibid.

17. Ibid.

18. Kate L. Turabian, *A Manual for Writers of Research Papers, Theses, and Dissertations: Chicago Style for Students and Researchers*, 7th ed. (Chicago: University of Chicago Press, 2007), 71.

19. Barry Lane and Gretchen Bernabei, *Why We Must Run With Scissors: Voice Lessons in Persuasive Writing 3–12* (Shoreham, VT: Discover Writing Press, 2001), 240.

20. Brian W., "The Answer to Stress," *Write It: Find Your Voice. Develop Your Craft. Publish Your Work*, http://teacher.scholastic.com/writeit/readpoem.asp?id=618&genre=Essay&Page=1&sortBy=.

21. Carolyn Davis, "The Story of an Athenaeum Spider," *Thinking Outside the Book: Essays for Innovative Librarians* (Jefferson, NC: McFarland Publishers, 2008), 170–174.

22. Joe Landsberger, *Study Guides and Strategies*, www.studygs.net/wrtstr6.htm.

23. Joanna Tarabia, "Transitional Words and Phrases," writing2.richmond.edu/writing/wweb/trans1.html.

24. Ibid.

25. Ibid.

26. Carolyn Davis, "A Research Slice of Life," in *Writing and Publishing: The Librarian's Handbook*, ed. Carol Smallwood (Chicago: ALA Editions, 2009).

27. Maxine Williams, editorial note to Carolyn Davis (June 21, 2009).

28. Linda Bridges and William F. Rickenbacker, *The Art of Persuasion: A National Review Rhetoric for Writers* (New York: National Review, 1991), 93. Bridges and Rickenbacker credit Edward P. J. Corbett, *Classical Rhetoric for the Modern Student* (New York: Oxford University Press, 1971) for the structure and argument of their chapter "Persuade Your Reader."

29. Ibid., 94–95.

30. Ibid., 95–96.

31. Ibid., 96–98.

32. Ibid., 98.

33. Ibid., 99.

34. Ivor Bowen, ed., *The Statues of Wales* (London: T. Fisher Unwin, 1908), 37.

35. R. R. Davies, *Conquest, Coexistence and Change: Wales 1063–1415 History of Wales*, Vol. 2 (New York: Oxford University Press, 1987), 463.

36. Ibid., 463.

37. Bureau of Public Affairs, "Kennan and Containment, 1947," *U.S. Department of State: Diplomacy in Action*, www.state.gov/r/pa/ho/time/cwr/17601.htm.

38. Ibid.

CHAPTER 2

Issues and Challenges

America has believed that in differentiation, not in uniformity, lies
the path of progress. It acted on this belief; it has advanced human
happiness, and it has prospered.

—*Louis D. Brandeis*

In this chapter, we look at some caveats or warnings—situations to be
aware of in persuasive writing and options to deal with them. Examples of
unusual structures in persuasive essays and letters are also provided.

THE AUTHOR'S CREDENTIALS AND CREDIBILITY

If you are researching a topic that includes interviews for a high school,
college, or graduate school report, it is important to establish credibility
with the people who you would like to be involved in your research, for
example, as participants or subjects. Your credentials as a person affiliated
with a legitimate high school or university will help to assure the prospective participants that you know what you are doing and have supervision.
You, your research supervisor, and the sponsoring school will be held responsible for your research methods and practices, so the people you contact about the research need to know who you are, what you intend to do,
why, and how.

A prudent plan is to ask for a letter of reference from your institution
that confirms your status. Accompany the letter with a written statement
of your own that you will confine your interview to the medium of your report, and keep confidential any other information that you gather that
doesn't relate to your report, such as telephone numbers, e-mail addresses,

and any extraneous or personal topics. You don't need the subject's permission to write as you see fit; however, it is advisable to deal with your subject honestly and with integrity.

If you are a professional writer, how do you present your credentials to an editor and, subsequently, to an audience, as an authority about a particular topic? Editors of magazines, journals, and books usually become acquainted with prospective authors through an introduction from other established authors and editors, book fairs, and written proposals that outline and describe the material (See "Strategies for Success"). Readers of magazines, journals and books become acquainted with authors through "about the author" blurbs, speaking engagements, and, in the cases of books, sometimes book launches and autograph sessions.

THE PERTINENCE OF THE TOPIC: WHAT TO DO WHEN THE SITUATION CHANGES

Sometimes the tone or structure of a topic will change as the author is writing a report or article. Current examples include the changes in positions of writers of economics and business articles from a couple of years ago to current leaner times.

There were many such instances in the late 1980s and early 1990s, as the Cold War between the United States and the Soviet Union collapsed, after having been a primary issue in many international situations for more than 40 years. Issues such as the containment of Soviet aggression and the effect of the East–West divide of Germany became much less significant very suddenly, although many of the economic issues remained, to be assumed by the European Union. What do you do when your topic goes absent without leave or is missing in action?

Whether you have built a career defining a particular perspective on an issue or are new to the practice of analyzing data, it is necessary to become familiar with the background of your issue and alternatives to your projected outcome. Not only will you appear to be a broad-minded, well-informed analyst, but you will also be ready from a position of authority to explain what has happened. In analyzing past events or attempting to predict future happenings, it is more effective to be well informed about the issues than to be committed to one viewpoint. See the chapter "Strategies for Success" for effective ways of gathering and imparting information.

ARE YOU THE FIRST ONE TO WRITE
THAT POINT OF VIEW IN THAT WAY?

The evils and basic definitions of plagiarism are explained in some detail in the chapter "Problems and Solutions." To protect yourself, be sure to document your sources and dates. These will provide references for anyone who may doubt your work's authenticity. Your teacher, supervisor, or editor will tell you which citation style is appropriate, and many manuals and books describe and give examples of particular styles, such as *The Chicago Manual of Style*, which is published by the University of Chicago and is generally favored for research essays and publications. The style manuals and guides published by Oxford University Press are other authoritative sources.[1] The proper citation of quotes, thoughts, and paraphrases from others' work and thoughts is very important. A person's words are his intellectual property," and intellectual property belongs to the person who thought of the concept. If you are using a phrase, sentence, paragraph, or concept that came from someone else, you must credit that person. Cite a source appropriately whenever you know you are quoting or paraphrasing from another source.

Citations should become a habit, like tooth brushing. Authors need not let the citation process frighten them from expressing their own perspectives and from researching creatively and distinctly. The use of citations is meant to share intellectual wealth and give credit to its originators.

HOSTILITY FROM TEACHERS, SUPERVISORS,
OR EDITORS

It is not unusual to encounter disagreement from those who review essays and presentations, for example, during reviews of academic theses and dissertations, and professional presentations, during which the author/presenter is or may be called upon to defend his or her research or perspective.

Additionally, in writing for publication, there are many phases during the publication process when an author may be called upon to explain or defend her or his work.

Hostility is a different situation. Its source may be any one or more issues that may be difficult for the author or presenter to know or find. First, try to identify a concrete problem by asking the person about it. Is your topic or written presentation on point and appropriate to the subject and format to which you agreed? Have you cited appropriately, according to the expectations of the person who is reviewing your work? Are you on deadline, or are you a day or two, week or two, or month or two, past the day without having communicated with the appropriate person? No one takes any of those mistakes lightly. If you have misunderstood some communication, try to clear it up before your work's due date. If you have truly made a mistake in collecting, citing, or presenting information, explain it to the person or group to whom you are responsible and include any evidence that supports something having honestly gone wrong. (For example, you forgot to include a signed permission slip to use another person's work, but you have scanned a copy of the slip into your hard drive. Whew.)

Do not try to use the excuses of being immature, being unprepared, or one that I heard many times as I edited university students' essays: being so busy (shopping and going to parties, presumably) that they didn't have time to consult their instructors or professors. Those are cop-outs and are not appropriate in professional environments (and I include high school and college as professional environments). Illnesses and other genuine emergencies are legitimate reasons. It is a good idea for students to provide documentation from some authority, such as a medical specialist, member of the clergy, or counselor. I remember a professor in college writing in the syllabus for his class that stress was not an acceptable reason for an extension; stress was a part of life. Many other professors and employers these days agree, as they have at least since the beginning of the Industrial Revolution. An exception might be made, however, if you have a medical condition that is exacerbated by stress. Again, provide documentation.

Sometimes you may encounter hostility from another person's agenda in an academic or a work environment that has no direct relation to your research or writing. If you seriously suspect incompetence, bigotry, or other problems that are the fault of the person or group to whom or which you have submitted your work, there are avenues of appeal both within and outside organizations. You need some courage to seek redress, but if you have evidence of incompetence, bigotry, or harassment, I encourage you to pursue your claim as far as you are able.

At times an effective way to deal with professional antagonism is to shift attention away from the subject that is under assault. This method can be especially effective in this era of faxes, e-mail, and instant messages, when expressions of emotions can be sent in minutes, and people may fire off communications without really thinking about or working on them. A few years ago I encountered a colleague who read a long essay of mine.

Initially, she almost liked it, but time and a variety of issues convinced her that she hated my work, which she stated with increasing fervor whenever called to comment upon it, until she reached a near-tantrum. During one of our rare exchanges, after she had gone on at length and with heat, I responded, "What did you think of the formatting?" It did not reconcile her to my essay, but it made her stop her tirade for a while and think more coherently.

PRESSURE

To relieve pressure, get to know the writing process that works best for you. Are you a planner who likes to get the work done before or just at deadline? Are you a person who learns quickly and gets work finished quickly, without much planning? Or do you prefer to work on your research and writing consistently, even if you are discouraged by slow or less than brilliant results? For large research projects, consistent work tends to yield better results than flashes of inspiration, especially when inspiration cannot be summoned at will and you have a deadline to meet. For presentations that are less dependent on research and outcomes, spontaneity can be an asset. Following are some questions to consider as you construct your essay: Does your initial assumption make sense and reflect the information about the subject that is available to you? Have you incorporated opposing views and the reasons behind them in your assessment of the subject? Do your transition paragraphs flow smoothly and sensibly? Does your conclusion make sense, and express what you intend to say?

DON'T FORGET TO BREATHE!

The process of collecting and synthesizing information requires time and patience. The writer must put it in a structure that makes sense and is correct in grammar and syntax. As William Kelleher Storey advises in *Writing History: A Guide for Students*, give yourself time and distance from your work to get a fresh perspective. Allow others to read and critique it to benefit from their points of view, which will be more objective than yours.[2] Because you are writing or presenting a persuasive piece, you need to be sure that readers or an audience will understand your work, that it is presented well, and that it is likely to have the desired effect. The opinion of others during the writing process is of tremendous importance. They are the document's first audience.

A persuasive piece may begin with the author's premise based on emotion. A presentation that is fact based is less subjective than one appealing principally to emotion and can be tremendously effective. Emotions can be regarded as sentimental and subjective, but documented facts are more difficult to dispute. Here is a small example:

Premise 1: We must not discriminate on the basis of wealth or privilege when choosing a candidate.

The supporting points: Merit needs to be the main consideration in choosing a candidate, because ability will be a significant factor in the candidate's success at the tasks.

A competent official is more likely to do the job effectively than an incompetent one.

Although wealth and privilege often imply power, and power helps to win elections, wealth and power do not imply competence for elected office. A better option for the wealthy may be the support of the chosen candidate's campaign.

Conclusion: The most competent candidates should be considered, rather than those whose main asset is wealth.

The supporting points explain why the writer has this premise and underscore the main reason why ability needs to be the primary consideration in choosing a candidate. This demonstrates another factor in persuasive art: the effectiveness of explaining your argument or point of view. An audience or reader wants to believe a presenter or writer has an open agenda—there should be no sense of secretive behavior or withholding. Readers are inclined to trust writers who are clear and honest, even if their arguments present a bias.

Following is an example of a five-paragraph essay: It begins with a topic sentence and follow-up statement that are followed by three paragraphs that supply facts and arguments to state the case further. The final paragraph states the conclusion.

WHY MARRIAGE IS NOT ALWAYS NECESSARY TO A WOMAN

Topic Sentence: "Married people are happier than those who are single." That statement applies to some married people, but the old-fashioned phrase "single blessedness" contains truth.

Supporting Point 1: An unmarried woman controls her own income. It is good to know that any money a woman makes is her own. She is not responsible for anyone else's support. Who hasn't wanted to be able to make significant purchasing decisions with her own money? An unmarried woman who supports herself has the social and financial freedom to budget for herself. If this sounds self-centered, remember that a woman who is on her own also has the luxury of giving to charity and volunteering time that is her own. These days, a woman need not marry for social acceptance or financial support. She may lose her job or otherwise lose money, but a husband would also be vulnerable to the effects of an economic downturn or other employment issues.

Supporting Point 2: A woman has more social and professional freedom now than in the past. In addition to increased professional opportunities, a single woman has many fewer restrictions now. An unmarried woman may buy a house, sail a boat around the world, or adopt or give birth to a child. Practices such as not granting a woman credit or discriminating against a single mother or her child are illegal now. A woman may have relationships that do not lead to marriage. This freedom to decide and develop the status of a relationship that is not based principally on social or financial necessity is liberating to each partner.

Supporting Point 3: A woman can be happy on her own. She likes maintaining her home for herself — cooking and decorating, for example — and knowing that anything that she puts into her living space will not be dirtied, eaten, or borrowed by someone else. At home or elsewhere a woman can pursue her own interests. Her time, possessions, and inclinations are her own. A woman can be sociable or solitary without having to consider the presence or absence of a spouse

Conclusion: An unmarried woman has latitude that can be fulfilling. She needs not to be governed by the restrictions of the past and can opt for a life that is stimulating, socially and professionally rewarding, and psychologically beneficial.

The final paragraph restates the topic using material from the three supporting paragraphs. This type of essay is succinct: focused and logical, it is direct and on-point.

EXAMPLES OF INTRODUCTIONS

Following are two examples of introductions of mine. These are not five-paragraph essays, but parts of longer works that use research, observation, and analysis to explain situations. The first is an introduction to a historical dissertation and describes some of the background of North Wales in the 14th century. The second is autobiographical.

The historical introduction sets the time and place. It describes the background of the subject—in this case, the English administration of North Wales from the late 13th to the early 14th century, C.E. It is longer and more detailed than many other essays and articles, and is part of a chapter of a book-length research project.

The autobiographical introduction also has a historical context, but it is recent history. The first paragraph sets a humorous tone as it describes general emotions about writing. The second paragraph mentions some of my specific conditions and experiences to focus the reader's attention on the autobiographical content.

ASPECTS OF POWER RELATIONSHIPS IN THE ENGLISH ADMINISTRATION OF WALES: 1282–1415

Introduction

The Principality of Wales in the 14th century was a land with a history of continual invasion; however, the northwest had natural barriers of estuaries and mountains that gave it more physical resistance to invasion than the south. The geography helped to develop a nation of separate and distinct political, religious, social, economic, and cultural identities. In the first century AD, long before its annexation to the Crown of England in 1284, Wales was occupied by the Romans. There followed a period of Anglo-Saxon aggression and internal struggle, Wales being divided among its petty kings. From post-Roman times onward, however, Welsh people formed and preserved their identity and Wales as a distinct entity, despite the threats to its survival from internal and external pressures and changing socioeconomic circumstances. Wales survived and maintained its distinctive features throughout the Middle Ages.

Additionally, Glyndŵr had Tudor cousins and had been educated in England. His father-in-law, David Hanmer, had been a solicitor and chief justice of the King's Bench, among other appointments in the Crown's administration. The family's interrelationships through marriage and political ties connect repeatedly between England and the principalities of North and South Wales, and the same was true of many others among the Welsh gentry, many of whom intermarried and were descendents of the same kin. Opposing that tradition of kinship legitimacy was the "usurper," Henry IV, who was a cousin of the royal line and could not claim direct descent.

Ultimately, it is not surprising that the Welsh gentry cooperated with the English administration after Wales was annexed by Edward III in 1284. The gentry were obliged to carve roles for themselves as they were inter-related with the English and the Welsh.

In a number of ways regarding military strength between England and the 14th century principality, the situation of synthesis or even of co-existence is that after the principality's annexation a stronger, manifold larger occupying presence was able to take it over and impose many of the Crown's requirements upon much of north and west Wales. Inspection of the social and administrative structures and main issues of the north and west principalities reveals much willingness among the gentry, as well as clergy, nobles and other participants, to cooperate and assist in the Crown's administration of it. To make the situation work for the Welsh of the principality, its own nobles and gentry had to be involved in its administration after annexation. The Welsh nobility and gentry, in their turn, were aware that if the principality were to survive, and in some ways thrive, they were obliged to guide the administration as the Crown directed, while they alternately maintained and developed the characteristics and structure of the land as they were able. Members of the gentry were rewarded in their turn with land and manors, political, military, and ecclesiastical offices for the men and their kin.

Realistically, greater power and influence were possible to the gentry through cooperation with and adaptation to English institutions, and many of the gentry assumed similar roles to the ones their ancestors had played for other conquerors. The roles ought not to be seen as traitorous to Wales as both the English and Welsh of this period were adapting to, changing, and being influenced by institutions that were themselves adapting to the principality of the 14th century.

We leave the 14th century now and return to modern challenges.

"How Much Time Do I Have?"

For writers, that question generally has more to do with editorial deadlines than with a person's actual life's length, although over time the former very probably has a significant impact upon the latter. In my own case, the phrase, "You promised (insert editor's name here) that you'd have the manuscript completed by (insert date here)" takes on a haunting, metallic quality, similar to Marley's ghost's bemoaning, "I wear the chains I forged in life." Nor does it help that I have been engaged in this pursuit for nearly 19 years and that, at any given moment, it seems sometimes, at least one of my (nonmusical) *opera* is being read and/or reviewed (!) by someone. What matters are the next deadline and the next critique.

The period of the 1960s to the 1990s was an interesting time to be a young person. Privileged in many ways, disadvantaged in others, normal in most, I grew up in America at a time when people with disabilities were beginning to be thought of by many people, but not by all, as integrated, complete human beings, rather than as disabilities with human characteristics. Since the late 1980s I have worked in international relations and research—the latter in Northern Ireland, Jamaica, and Wales. I was born in 1960, and therefore I was just the age to be a guinea pig in many aspects of education, employment, and international living.

Following are three example introductions for works of first-person reporting that present persuasive arguments and are written from biased perspectives: The first vignette demonstrates four examples of representatives of groups that experienced disenfranchisement in Turkey and how each worked out adjustments or solutions to each the issue, outside and within the First European Conference on Peacemaking and Conflict Resolution. The second report describes my memories of my experiences in Northern Ireland in 1992–1993 on the first day of the Good Friday Agreement of 1998. The third describes the issue of an inebriated speaker at a conference of reporters and diplomats who were speaking about situations in Haiti. Each uses first-person reporting, which is the description of personal experiences, to tell a true story. The unfolding of events as they happened is used as a method of persuasion. The readership is expected to feel and react in particular ways in response to the stories.

PEACE CONFERENCE IN TURKEY

Ethnic Self-Determination: French and Other Resolutions

Carolyn Davis

In 1992, I first embarked as an international representative in my own right. My first experience was that of a delegate to the First European Conference on Peacemaking and Conflict Resolution in Ankara, Turkey. My closest friend from the Institute of Conflict Analysis and Resolution at

George Mason University in Fairfax, Virginia, was to be there, too. Ankara was her home city, and her mother, whom I had met previously, could join us for a few outings and a meal. The flight from Washington, D.C., to Istanbul included a stopover in Germany, where I was treated with extreme and somewhat commanding courtesy, which included my being driven to my connecting flight in a van used to transport people with mobility impairments.

"Well, if it's all going to be this easy . . ." I thought, as the plane breezed toward the East, which demonstrated the folly of complacency before the fact. My first stage in Istanbul was a mild interrogation, but then, I was a foreigner, so expected a few questions.

"Why are you here? What do you want? Is there anyone here to meet you?" hammered out the person I assumed to be a customs agent.

"I am here to attend a peace conference in Ankara," I replied, in a tone dignified enough for the late secretary of state, Charles Evans Hughes. "No one is meeting me."

"How are you going to get there?" If I had been in a somewhat better mood, I would have asked her for a ride. But why tempt fate?

"Are there taxis outside?" I asked, allowing myself some testiness.

"Yes," she conceded unwillingly.

"Then I will take one of those," I said decisively, to indicate that my part in this pas de deux was over. In Turkey, people with disabilities were often treated as subhuman. Quite honestly, I hadn't been exposed to such blatant discrimination mixed with hatred in many years.

After a fairly harrowing ride in a taxi, I arrived at the hotel where the conference and the delegates had been booked. After a few anxious moments I realized that the wheelchair did fit through both the hotel and bathroom doors. I then descended in the elevator to await the convocation of the conference. To my delight, the dining room's menu featured not only the fairly standard beer and wine, but also a choice of freshly squeezed orange juice, or vanilla, strawberry, or chocolate milk shakes, each in five-ounce glasses. It was a delight to discover how pleasant a small milk shake can be, after the daily sessions were finished and yet two hours before dinner.

The sessions were to begin that night, and an initial bit of disruption occurred because a delegation from France appeared to want to boycott the conference because there would be no presentations in French. Thinking it might alleviate the tension a little, I wheeled over to the delegation.

"Bon soir, mon français, ç'est terrible," I conceded, feeling that we could at least begin with an agreement on something. Anyway, they were smiling and saying, *"Non, non,"* which was diplomatic of them. I continued, *"Bien sur, s'il vous plait, voulez-vous se pour asseoir avec moi?"* (Where, *sans doute,* we would continue this profound, diplomatic exchange.) I seriously hoped I wasn't destroying whatever Franco-Anglo-American goodwill there might have remained in the room. To my amazement, the French delegation returned to their table and spent the rest of the conference politely participating in English. Were they afraid that if they didn't I'd go over and *parler* again? Or was it respect and legitimacy that they had sought, and had received from my much less than university-level attempts? I don't know, but chalk that experience up to that you very often can relate on a human level, even besides a community or national one.

Several of the issues on the agenda concerned ethnic self-determination. One day a young man stood up in one of the sessions and announced that he was breaking the law: he was half-Kurdish and half-Turkish. The law had been broken because it was illegal in Turkey to mention the Kurdish people as a legitimate group, and to identify yourself as one was not allowed. It was stimulating, and about time for someone in this conference to present the issue. Another example of bravery and "faith in the process," as another delegate expressed it later, was an Armenian woman's declaring herself Armenian and talking openly about the Armenian genocide of 1917; discussion of that event was also illegal in Turkey.

My part in the process was restricted, because the feedback from the initial agenda was that there was an excess of American involvement in the European conference. Compared with many of the delegates, I was a neophyte; my international experiences were ahead of me. I was impressed at the depth of exchange at this conference. My previous experiences with conferences had been that information was exchanged and sometimes programs reached an embryonic stage of development, but no one had ever risked arrest to declare an identity or other points of ethnic determination. However those situations were to be evaluated by political or socioeconomic standards, it had taken the presenters' personal courage and faith to state them. Positive societal change is engendered by courage and faith, which in turn bolsters the courage and faith of others, encouraging and directing them to work for change, and so, as examples, the Civil Rights Act of 1964 was passed and the conflicts in Vietnam and Cambodia were ended.

The structure of the preceding essay follows the form of introduction, examples, and conclusion concerning how societal issues encountered in the conference were addressed. The report of the essay is followed by analysis that directs the reader to certain conclusions. Its structure is similar to that of "Strathmore House and Other Issues of Jamaica" (see Chapter 4: "Strategies for Success"); however, "Peace Conference in Turkey" contains more narrative and invites the reader to experience the process without as much author input.

APRIL 10, 1998, MEDIATION AND SOME EXAMPLES OF POWER

Carolyn Davis

I had hit a personal-most record early in the afternoon with a temperature of 103 degrees Fahrenheit. As I was lying in bed feeling a heat glaze resting upon and within me, I wondered vaguely where Em, the feline commander of our household in Kingston, Jamaica, was keeping herself. I decided she must be either on our patio or—technically not allowed but in fact indulged in repeatedly by our two pounds of kitten stubbornness—lying on the kitchen table. Another thought—that I ought to make my way to the bathroom sometime in the next few hours—occupied my mind as well, and I felt a pang of remorse to discover while sitting up that Em was actually holding a vigil for my aching, overheated self. She was stationed at the end of the bed, wearing her hooded look that bespoke either anger or concern. Subsequent to my crawling back to bed after my long, slow journey to the adjoining room, she peered into my eyes at hourly intervals, to retreat to the end of the bed and the hooded look in between.

At different times during the preceding week I had felt physically good and bad, finally sliding into feeling terrible on the previous day with either a case of flu or Dengue fever. My Peace Corps housemate, ever the newshound, had turned on CNN when she arrived home on the evening of April 10. The reports were glowing: in London people were stopping traffic to give each other cheer, and the participants in the Good Friday Agreement were announcing the great news on the great day.

"Oh, that's good," I muttered to myself with as much enthusiasm as I could with my fever. "I hope that it lasts." A few days later, after the fever diminished, I read the story of the Good Friday Agreement and for 20 minutes cried for joy.

Peace between the communities would have been difficult to envision in Coleraine and Stroke City (Londonderry/Derry) five to six years before, when I was there to do research. The latter city was so named generally according to which community a person belonged—Protestant or Catholic.

Small communities may become significantly sectarian, and sectarian division breeds classic symptoms of dysfunction among people who are encouraged to remain isolated from one another. Myths, legends, and their misinformation contribute to the problems. Separation is part of the process of dysfunction; meeting and talking ameliorates the dysfunction to some degree. I had gone to Northern Ireland in September 1992 for an internship that had been approved by Professor Christopher Mitchell of the Center (now Institute) of Conflict Analysis and Resolution at George Mason University and Professor Seamus Dunn of the Centre for the Study of Conflict in Coleraine, Northern Ireland.

Note that the description and build-up construct an effective persuasive paragraph through illustration, that "A" leads to "B," "B" leads to "C," and "D" succeeds "C."

I interviewed community leaders and participated in mediation sessions between young people from two sixth forms (the British equivalent of 12th grades) who were from different communities. The process was indeed educational as the barriers between them were at first reinforced, then significantly broken down by varied communication ways and means, including game playing and the eventual sharing of stories of our lives, as we mediators participated in the process, too. A particularly bonding episode was the disclosure by two girls, one from each group, that their fathers had died when each was six. When they prayed, they envisioned their fathers. This similarity of practice was quite a breakthrough between the groups. It was a significant episode in the young people's realization that they had some issues, practices, hopes, and beliefs in common.

Note that the issue in the above paragraph might be with people who had lived in or experienced the community situations in the early 1990s. This report was obviously written after the fact, for people who have been outside the situation.

An interesting question that I received was pitched when I went to someone's house for dinner and upon meeting me a teenager asked, "How
would you escape from a concentration camp?" It was a school project
for him. That kind of challenge is not asked every day!

I replied that a strategy of the administration of concentration camps
was chaos: if the prisoners could not count on anything, it was a deter-
rent to their organizing to revolt or escape, so he should plan for chaos.

After my internship finished, I moved to Londonderry to take courses
and continue my research; however, I returned home in February 1993.
There were then, as ever, many points of view about "the Troubles" and
how to attempt to deal with them. Ones that I felt were practical and valid
demystified the situation and brought people together who had a lot in
common. Meeting people on common ground or helping in that facili-
tation could be dangerous. Corrymeela, a mediation center in the town of
Ballymena, had a huge mural in one of its meeting rooms. The mural was
of a tree with many leaves attached to it. Each leaf represented a mediator
who had been killed.

This paragraph states some empirical information that follows up on
statements two paragraphs earlier. The sixth-form students had been taught
that neither England nor Ireland wanted to assume the issues of Northern
Ireland; meeting at Corrymeela had facilitated their being able to communicate with one another; the description of the huge mural is a detail
that helps set the scene and convey the danger involved.

Corrymeela had a particularly effective strategy to entice participants to
complete their programs. A professional chef cooked two marvelous meals
a day, with a choice of vegetarian or not. The enticement of excellent food
and regular breaks in the proceedings—coffee, tea, and biscuits were
frequently available, too—were appreciated by hungry and tired peace-
seekers.

The time at the mediation center was an educational respite that provided some glimpses of hopeful possibilities, but soon the grimmer reality
of the then-current situation hit—literally. On Friday, November 13, 1992,
a huge bomb stalled holiday shopping considerably, as it devastated Coleraine's business district. The blast could be felt through a door handle
inside a building about one mile away from ground zero. The vibration began slowly, then built to a crescendo and subsided. It was the first major

bombing in Coleraine in approximately 16 years. It was a long way from November 1992 to April 1998.

After my experiences in Northern Ireland I felt that although some progress was occurring among individuals, the realpolitik of the issues could not be settled anytime soon. I cheered the advances of the later 1990s that culminated in the Good Friday Agreement, and mourn that recent progress in Northern Ireland is likely attributable to other acts of terrorism and protest in the world, more than actual concurrence among the parties regarding the issues within Northern Ireland.

The Good Friday Agreement was made more imperative once the prime ministers of Great Britain and Northern Ireland and Ireland declared that neither country would continue to support the destruction in Northern Ireland either financially, politically, or emotionally. America's zero tolerance of terrorist activities and the respect that was shown to member of Parliament Gerry Adams, the leader of the political party Sinn Fein and a leader of the peace process, seemed to facilitate the Irish Republican Army's decommissioning of its weapons. However, it was the unequivocal statements by Tony Blair and Bertie Ahern that persuaded—perhaps, more accurately, demanded—an end to the violence. The prime ministers were exercising their political power to demand that a long-term political issue that affected quite a few countries come to an end. As previously mentioned, the use of power has a great deal of significance in the effectiveness of persuasion.

There have been attempts for decades to develop theories of conflict, principally through those of needs and economics.[3] For example, Professor Kenneth Boulding, a world-famous economist who was a founder of the United States Institute of Peace, and truly brilliant consultant to the Center for the Study of Conflict at George Mason University during the late 1980s, emphasized the importance of interconnected systems. His economics theories were multidimensional. Boulding emphasized the importance of "ecodynamics" to the understanding of human behavior in many spheres. Ecodynamics deals with subtle, humanitarian influences in society. Boulding believed humans were doomed unless people developed appropriate social science research, and he presented this in historical and modern contexts within conflict theory. He then defined power in three categories: destructive, productive, and integrative. Boulding also addressed the basic social structures of power. He argued that power in groups tends to be hierarchical.[4] Examples of power structures include nations and the ownership of land. Occasionally, power will be exercised for its own sake, without any object. Sometimes the object of a person's exercise of one type of power, such as force, is to increase her ability to exercise other types of power, such as integrative. Anwar Sadat's metamorphosis from youthful freedom fighter to president of Egypt is an example, as is Gerry Adams's political biography.

Boulding claimed that integrative power is potentially the most significant form of power, although difficult to define. He saw respect, along with love, as examples of integrative power. Respect is closely related to legitimacy. The creation and maintenance of individuals' identities depends on the integrative system in a society. Individuals develop their particular identities at least in part by gaining the respect and acknowledgment of others.[5]

According to Boulding, destructive power plays two main roles in society. Destruction may be the first stage in a productive process, or it may be used to intimidate and hurt. The military is a prime example of an organization of destructive power for this second role. Boulding noted that while destructive power is needed to make threats, threats become most effective when made in a context that is integrative and legitimates the demand for submission.

Boulding described integrative power thus: "A major source of the integrative power of a community or organization is the degree to which the personal identity of the members involved is bound up with their perception of the identity of the community or organization as a whole."[6]

Boulding further made the point in *Three Faces of Power* that when combined with human organizations and their diversity, anyone's identification with groups can lead to intergroup or intercommunal conflicts.[7]

In a historical context, and as an illustration of the constructive work of groups through time, Boulding made a well-known (and often quoted) point that at least 90 percent of human activity, even in the modern age, was/is peaceful and productive—including raising food and children and building communities.[8] Boulding also had theories of social dynamics that cultures do not develop ideologies: the true test of an ideology is to establish and maintain a culture around it, as to be functional an ideology must inspire people with security and a sense of their place in the world.[9]

Criminologists George Vold and Thomas Bernard, who influenced Richard Quinney,[10] evaluated conflict in terms of subgroups and criminal behavior, particularly in terms of "in-groups" and "out-groups": the former are likely to make the laws and the latter to engage in what in-groups define as criminal behavior. There are many research projects concerning

Northern Ireland's situations of conflict, and many excellent research specialists were based at the Centre for the Study of Conflict, including its director, Seamus Dunn.

Among presentation issues and nightmares, here is one that occurred during a convocation that I had helped to plan and a presentation by an intoxicated speaker.

A presenter's principal responsibilities include: being properly prepared, arriving and presenting on time, staying within the time limit, and being sure that she or he is speaking about the assigned topic.

About 13 years ago I encountered a speaker who presented problems at a mini-conference. Most guests were quite accommodating and easy to work with, but one American was exceedingly high maintenance. He made several demands that were well beyond those of his conference colleagues. The worst issue, however, was that the speaker came to his presentation somewhat inebriated. This is an issue that proves a challenge to any presenter's reputation, as well as the sponsor's, not to mention its effect on the speaker's health, reliability, and authority. A person who is under the influence of alcohol or other drugs behaves in ways that are disrespectful and embarrassing to the other speakers and the guests. A presenter needs to be sober.

PRESENTATIONS IN GENERAL

Another issue of public life is the demanding, harassing audience. There are times when speakers may need to be kept on topic and accountable for their "spin" (White House press conferences come to mind) and times when an audience needs to back off and the presenter needs to take control of the situation. An example of the latter happens when a guest speaker very appropriately says, "Now, just one more question on (this subject), and then let us go to another topic." A guest presenter is, after all, a guest, who is appearing at a person or group's request. The person's presence is not compulsory. Although the audience may desire strongly to wring information from an unwilling speaker, there are many times when it is inappropriate to try to run someone to ground in an effort to extract information.

THE ADDITIONAL POWER OF THE MEDIA

The reasons for the media presenting an issue or perspective, and the ways in which it accomplishes this, can be fascinating. Journalism exists in many forms, with any degree of interpretation of relatively accurate truths from cogent to nonexistent and from tracked, quoted, and cited conscientiously to made up completely.

Advertisements from 60 to 100 years ago are some of my favorite examples of truly creative writing. Exaggerations that are farcical were presented to the public in the forms of advertisements of enticing display, as they are today. The ancient Latin phrase, caveat emptor, "Let the buyer beware," needs to be at the front of people's minds as we listen to or read advertisements from any era.

When analyzing the claims of an advertisement, or writing one, make certain of your sources, and beware, or be aware, of creative journalism. Sensitive information has the power to damage or destroy someone's reputation or career, and you need your sources to be reliable and informed. Be aware of the presentation of facts that tends to occur in advertisements and other testimonials. The goal of a contemporary advertisement is to entice readers or listeners to buy the product, but not to create grounds for a lawsuit. Look at the example of an ad for Sloppo soap, a fictitious product.

GET READY TO BLAST DIRT OUT OF THE WATER WITH SLOPPO SOAP!

Since 1850, Sloppo has used the highest-quality hog fat and kerosene to address all of the cleaning needs of a busy household. There is no need to buy separate soap and laundry detergent—Sloppo cleans everything.

This wonderful cleaning product must be stored away from direct light or flame and must not be swallowed. The Sloppo Company guarantees that it will get any sort of residue or substance off anything—from skin to tin to car engines. Don't worry about quality—Sloppo's safety seal keeps it fresh and strong for at least four years of normal use. If you see bubbles, shards of sandpaper, or other signs of tampering, return the product to the Sloppo Company for replacement. You can order Sloppo soap in packages of five and ten cakes directly from our Web site.

After a busy afternoon cleaning your carburetor with Sloppo, you can get your hands and yourself just as grime-free. Since 1960 we have incorporated hypoallergenic perfume and lanolin mixed with cold cream into Sloppo's detergent base. Be assured that it is gentle and effective for your hands and face—and tough enough for your grimiest challenges.

In these difficult times, reach for Sloppo—The Soap that Can Multitask!

The author explains that Sloppo soap uses the highest-quality ingredients and lists and describes the main ingredients that, according to the text, have been used since the soap was first made in 1850.

This ad is structured for readers. Words, not pictures, are its medium. The ad reminds the reader of the longevity of the Sloppo Company, then provides facts and even how-to information about the soap's multiple (questionable) uses. In addition to serving as a hand-and-body soap, Sloppo may be used as a crude oil solvent and laundry detergent. The Sloppo Company seeks to assure readers that purchasing this product is particularly wise during difficult economic times.

The ingredient information is structured to be reassuring about the multiple uses of Sloppo, although it is advisable with any important product information from an ad to conduct your own research to verify the statements. A reader may also be unwilling to buy the product in bulk and may want to ask a local store whether individual cakes of soap are available for purchase, instead of buying the larger amount online.

Now ask yourself, do you want a product whose manufacturer claims that it is safe and effective for everything from skin to car engines? Isn't it worth spending some money to assure yourself that your car and skin remain intact? As absurd as the Sloppo ad is, no small numbers of actual ads make claims that are nearly as absurd. Most ads are structured in small, quick ostentatious formats that are geared to convince you to buy a product or service. Protect yourself by evaluating the advertisement for its real message. What is it offering? What is it promising? Does it mention risks and make any guarantees in case of unfulfilled promises? Is the product beneficial to or healthy for you, can you afford it and, ignoring the advertisement's claim and conducting your own investigation, do you really want it? Ads come in many forms, including book reviews, but they should not be your sole reason for making a significant purchase.

Persuasive writers can develop their skills by analyzing others' persuasive writing as readers.

Following is a description of the poet Emily Dickinson that, although subjective, is based on empirical evidence to lend authority to the writer's evaluation. Notice that the writer begins with the conclusion that others state, according to the paragraph, and concludes with authors Vincent Wilson Jr.'s and Gale S. McClung's own evaluation.

> One of America's greatest poets—the verdict many critics and scholars have reached after reading hundreds of poems . . . [that] Dickinson had written but never published.

Ten poems were published during her lifetime. [Dickinson's] poetic techniques . . . anticipated twentieth century developments in poetry.[11]

In the full page of text from which the quotation is taken, the authors briefly describe the large collection of Dickinson's poems that was published after her death in 1886. The first volume was published in 1890, then another volume in 1891, and another in 1896. A collection of letters was published as well.[12] The authors give a brief background of Dickinson's family life and, to add depth and scope to their one-page essay, mention a behavior change when she became reclusive toward the end of her life.[13] The review of Dickinson's work combines informative historical background with a brief critique that instructs and, therefore, has a persuasive effect upon the reader. The writer who states an opinion is well advised to incorporate some data to support it.

Now let's move to a persuasive description of the enactment of a federal law in the 20th and 21st centuries in an excerpt from a recent presentation to a group of librarians:

The ADA [Americans with Disabilities Act of 1990] basically flips on its head the former concept that most people with disabilities are incapable of participating in society. It makes the statement that most people can, and that all of society should, participate to everyone's benefit.

Do not look on the ADA as a vehicle of fear . . . It is intended as a vehicle of inclusion . . . that many people with disabilities can function in society. In previous years, the onus was on the person who was disabled to adapt and adjust in order to function in the mainstream. Now society is sharing that responsibility in terms of physical and psychological access. Essentially the message of the Act is that what can be done, should be done.[14]

In the preceding example, an audience that knew very little about the Americans with Disabilities Act was instructed in its philosophy and user friendliness through the use of historical reference and instruction, as in the Dickinson example. The final sentence of the paragraph was the final sentence of the presentation, and one person in the audience said it was the phrase that she would report; evidently it summed up the presentation to her.

Media that seek to persuade us as consumers and lifetime students are everywhere these days. They can be useful tools of information as long as we retain awareness that we are being persuaded, even coerced, by the messages, and we control our reactions and are responsible for the consequences of our actions.

WHAT IS KNOWN VERSUS
WHAT IS INTERPRETED

Whenever a source is cited that is not the author's or presenter's own, there are levels of removal that involve filters and interpretations by the reader/researcher that are different from direct knowledge. Although citing information from written sources is a standard and accepted way of incorporating information in an essay or presentation, it is important to understand the difference between the author's unique research and the interpretation of others' work.

Historical research involves many degrees of removal, since it is beyond anyone's living memory. Sir Thomas Malory's literature about his interpretation of the history of Britain is an example of work that manufactured a story that was believed for a long time by some to be legitimate. It provides a lesson from medieval times about the importance of checking the validity of sources, although the ability of literate people to check sources was significantly more restricted than it is for contemporary researchers. Bards and poets were the public relations "Mad Men" of ancient, medieval, and early modern times. They were experts in the uses of persuasion to influence power. They had a significant impact on the events of their day through their uses of prophecy and verse. Some of their influence remains in the literature of Arthur, Merlin, and the stories of Welsh battles.

POWER RELATIONSHIPS IN THE PRINCIPALITY
OF WALES 1282–1415: BARDS AND POETS

The medieval bards of the 14th-century principality of Wales were elite men who weaved stories, satire, poetry, and prophecy for their patrons. Of the texts of prophecy from the Middle Ages in Britain that are extant, five are relatively well known. They are *Prophecia Merlini,* which was in private collections until the mid-20th century, and *The Last Kings of the English, The Holy Oil of St Thomas, Lilium Regnums,* and *Bridlington.* Among the works that can be defined as fabricated history is 12th-century clergyman[15] Geoffrey of Monmouth's *Historia Regum Britanniae,* or *History of the Kings of Britain,* of which *The Last Kings of the English* is a book.[16]

Geoffrey's *History,* which purports to tell the story of the Britons, ranges from an ancient group of wandering Trojans, to questionable leaders such as Lud, to the actual "emperor or pretender Constantine [III],"[17] to the arrival of the Angles and Saxons in the fifth century at the invitation of King Vortigen. Following accounts of Arthur's birth, fostering, and awareness that he is the heir of Uther Pendragon, who was one of the sons of Constantine, Arthur launches a campaign against the Saxons and extends his territory to Ireland, the Orkneys, Iceland, Norway, and Gaul.[18] Finally, after some exploits that may have been taken from stories of the Emperor Maximus of Britain, proclaimed in 383,[19] Arthur receives a critical (however, evidently, not permanent!) wound during battle in Cornwall and in AD 542 disappears to the magical island of Avalon to be healed. Geoffrey of Monmouth finally relates the recovery of the Anglo-Saxons as a result of British vices and of their downfall during the time of King Cadwaladr. However, in the *Prophecies of Merlin,* Geoffrey wrote a long poem of Arthur's mystical mentor, based on ancient Welsh poetry, and described Arthur's existence in "the Isle of the Blest," or Avalon.

Geoffrey's enthusiastic but basically fictitious and perhaps satiric story constructed a complete history for the descendants of the original Britons.[20] It has been argued controversially that the *History* created a past for them equal in legend to that of France, and gave hope for the future in the form of Merlin's prophecies of the second coming of King Arthur for the liberation of Wales. Gillingham suggests, however, that Geoffrey's interest may have been much more in the Anglo-Norman elite interests than the Welsh, and that the *History* has multiple ambiguities, such as its dedications, and that the kings of England would have looked at it as mainly a piece of propaganda.[21] According to historian Geoffrey Ashe, the *History* was "believed by all but a few skeptics."[22] Gillingham states, however, that it was regarded as "highly dubious" propaganda until the late 12th century.[23]

Historian John Gillingham acknowledges historian Christopher Brooke's interpretation that Geoffrey of Monmouth intended *The History* as parody, and yet another interpreter, Valerie Flint, believed the purpose behind the parody was "to exalt non-monastic views and styles of life."[24] Gillingham then states his own view that given the extensive political and military content of the work, its theme owed much to the "politics of cultural nationalism."[25] Author David Carpenter mentions the biography of Gruffudd ap Cynan that describes Gruffudd as another Arthur, contributing perhaps to the patriotism that the Welsh of the North felt and expressed in the mid-twelfth century. The Anglo-Norman surveys of the 1150s recorded the Welsh people saying openly and confidently that "by means of Arthur they will have the island back (and) call it Britain again."[26]

Another book of prophecy that has survived the centuries is the "Black Book of Carmarthen," which links to Geoffrey of Monmouth's *History of the Kings of Britain.* In his fictional account, Geoffrey of Monmouth first gave a prophet the name of Myrddin and connected him with the town of Carmarthen.[27]

First-person narrative is effective in recalling contemporary events and is truly effective in persuasive speaking and writing. When people who were part of it relay information about a historical event, they add verisimilitude—truth—to a situation. First-person narrative can be especially useful in the evaluation of historical events, as the participants not only tell the story but also evaluate its significance from the perspective of time.

Following is an excerpt from a summary of episode five, "Wounded Knee," of the PBS documentary *We Shall Remain.* The documentarians asked a variety of persons to assess the importance of Wounded Knee:

> **Robert Warrior, writer,** Osage Nation: The good that came out of Wounded Knee was the entry into American Indian political life of people who had not been there before, who had not had a real voice. People learned they could tackle problems, create opportunities. And I think that coming out of Wounded Knee, people knew they could make a difference.
>
> **Ken Tiger, former American Indian Movement (AIM) member,** Seminole tribe: There was a lot of sense of 'we're important and we can do something within our own people, our own tribe, our own homes.' I didn't go back to what I was doing before. I felt maybe I can do something to help, not only my people, but other people, too.
>
> **Narrator:** Native activism would spur the revitalization of Native cultures. In the years following the siege at Wounded Knee, Indians would create tribal schools and cultural institutions charged with preserving Indian traditions—and passing them on.
>
> **Paul Chaat Smith, writer,** Comanche Nation: In the late 60s and early 70s, these were still emerging ideas about reconnecting with traditional culture, language, religion that was starting to happen. But this became the majority sentiment in the space of just a handful of years. It was really about identity. It was about affirming we're still here, we want to be here, and we want to be here on our own terms.
>
> **John Trudell, former AIM leader,** Santee Sioux tribe: Whatever went on in the 60s and 70s, it's an extension, it's a continuation. It was no different

than what King Phillip was about, or Crazy Horse was about. And [by] whatever means and manner we could, since the Europeans arrived here, we've had to fight for our survival.

Charlotte Black Elk, Oglala historian, Oglala Lakota tribe: What the 1973 occupation did was people started saying "Hey, we're Indians. It's okay to be Indian. We are Indian, we really should be who we are." The struggle that we have in the 21st century is to remain ourselves. Every one of us has to do our part to remain Lakota, to remain Indian and to teach our children, to teach our grandchildren and make sure that there will be children sitting in sweat lodge, standing at the sun dance in a thousand years.[28]

These narratives summarized a series that presented significantly different perspectives from many sources of the 1970s. The combination of the perspective of 36 years with the participants' thoughts, contributed to the value of the documentary.

A VIGNETTE OF A COUPLE OF "JUMP-CHALLENGED" PEOPLE

Many years ago, I went parachute jumping with a man who was a swim coach for a club in North Carolina. It was the first jump for both of us, and each of us faced his or her own challenges. It took me two years of writing letters and making telephone calls to persuade him to make the parachute jump by using the approach that if we go together, we will be company for each other. The coach did not respond that we might be company for each other on the way to the emergency room or morgue, writing only, "If anything happens to you, your mother will *kill* me!" To which I responded that I was an adult and made my own decisions; many people jumped safely.

"Shouldn't we grow old gracefully?" he responded.

"It would be a once in a lifetime experience," I responded, in letters. This type of exchange went on for two years, not because I was an obsessive persuader who could not let go of a situation, but because Peter did not tell me the real reason he didn't want to jump: he is afraid of heights. He told me on the day we were to take our lessons for the jump, during the ride to the school.

Finally he wrote, "OK, if you go, *I* go." Thinking back, I realize he didn't specify where we might be going.

Talk about a challenge!

When Peter found a jump school and instructor for us, the instructor's only question, as we had not met, pertained to my weight. He was reassured when told I weigh only about 87 pounds, not the 240 that was his maximum. Because I am disabled, the instructor and I were obliged to make a tandem jump, so my weight was a significant factor.

The instructor demonstrated a tremendously positive attitude. His willingness to undertake our adventure was inspirational and educational in the challenges, rewards, and fun of reasonable risks.

Another example of persuasion in recreation relates to bird-watching. How do bird-watchers, know what they are seeing when birds are on the wing and a couple of miles off? It has a lot to do with the species they *expect* to see, but there can be major surprises, and an experienced bird aficionado must be alert to possibilities, such as an Icelandic duck that is suddenly found emigrating to the New England coast because of storms. I, however, have not proceeded past the "cigar ash" stage; that is, when every sighting that makes the birding pros and mavens (Raven-maven? Raving-maven?) hearts a-flutter, look to the novice like cigar ashes varying only slightly in size.

In January 1976, I either asked or was asked (probably a bit of each) to join my birder brother and a devoted birder friend of his on an expedition to Florida. I had to write a history term paper and wanted to read *All Creatures Great and Small*, and I suppose I thought the latter could be considered my contribution to the enumeration and preservation of wildlife. As it developed, I think my brother thought my almost unceasing laughter while reading the book might frighten the birds, but he and his friend managed to spot quite a few, as I recall. He also tried to instill in me some knowledge of the art and craft of birding. The only aspect that has stayed with me, however, is the part about being still. The rest of my birding is similar to my bridge playing—I can catch on to the major points if needed but have not found it practical to study.

A major reason why I do not aspire to be a birder is the time they have to arise early. The dear little beings (the birds, I mean) begin their day sometime around 4:00–4:30 A.M., and the serious birder must as well to catch their calls. In my truly productive teen years I was obliged to rise at 4:45 every school day from the autumn of 1976 to late spring of 1978 because our city high school was on double sessions and the juniors and seniors had the first shift. I promised myself after that that I would not regularly rise before 7 A.M. again, and I have kept that promise. I know many very productive people who rise with or before the sun; however, that way for me leads to massive fatigue and migraines, no matter how early I try to get to bed. At first, I thought I might have some luck with the late-rising birds, such as owls, but not so far. There was one instance in Aberystwyth, Wales, when I saw an obviously trained hawk tracking prey and returning to his trainer in the way designated by the practice. Although it is now a modern sport or hobby, its origins are in the Middle Ages, at least.

"Hawking!" I cried exultantly, in reference to the practice, not the professor, nor the selling of wares.

"It's called 'falconry,' actually," responded my taxi driver with such an autocratic, bored air of a specialist instructing an inferior being that I almost laughed.

"We always called it 'hawking,'" I replied, probably too generally, (because I was thinking of T.H. White's book *The Once and Future King* more than anything else). I gave the halfway-accurate impression that I referred in apostrophe to those I had read who knew something about it—in America. "Look at the beauty of the line that the bird is making."

This mellowed the driver a bit and he admitted the bird knew his onions, or had been well trained, obviously, in his phrase. While I can't say that on the strength of this we became friends, I guess the driver assumed as we watched that I wasn't totally ignorant of the sport. Although the bird's hunting becomes the enjoyment for humans of a blood sport, and that gory aspect cannot be ignored, a well-trained hawk or falcon in performance is a truly beautiful sight. The process involves total cooperation between human and bird.

TO OUTLINE OR NOT TO OUTLINE: WHAT ARE THE QUESTIONS?

Many authors of writing guides emphasize the practical uses of an outline. Some writers do not work without them; others do not work with them. They can be necessary tools to those who need to work out their structures in detail. They are useful guides for reference but need not be followed slavishly.

For example, the author wants to state the premise but leave some room to develop the plan. This strategy is useful in presentations when the presenter is not certain of the audience's familiarity with the topic. In this case, a presenter with a tightly developed outline will have to depart from the structure, so a looser plan or options for plans "B" and "C" are advisable in an outline. If you are comfortable with your topic, you may find that you favor the freedom to adapt your talk to the structure of a written speech; however, notes for important facts and dates may help you to avoid stage fright.

Following is an example of an outline, based on the analytical essay of William Kelleher Storey,[29] with persuasive aspects added by me.

ANALYTICAL:

   I.   Introduction: the background of the subject and your point of view.
      A.   The specific sources of your information
      B.   The conflicting opinions

  II.   Specific examples relevant to your essay.
      A.   Discuss any relevant history of the topic, including brief biographies and background information of the people involved. (This example is from "Peace Conference in Turkey" "My closest friend from the Institute of Conflict Analysis and Resolution at George Mason University in Fairfax, Virginia was to be there too. Ankara was her home city, and her mother, whom I had met previously, could join us for a few outings and a meal.")
      B.   Explain and evaluate perspectives on the topic.
          1.   What went on during the peace conference? (A. The self-identification of the "half-Turkish, half-Kurdish speaker; B. The presentation about the Armenian genocide)

 III.   Conclusion: The outcome or desired outcome (What happened?)
      A.   B. etc. Discuss the specific ways and means to obtain or enable the desired outcome. (Why did it happen?)[30]

BUILD AN ARGUMENT BY PRESENTING FACTS

Here are excerpts from a historical essay I wrote that presents examples of the English and Welsh administration of Wales that occurred during several years after King Edward III annexed Wales in 1284 for his own use. My persuasive argument was that the cooperation of the Welsh gentry with the English administration ought to be viewed as the gentry's attempt to preserve Welsh culture and tradition and was not traitorous to Wales.

ASPECTS OF POWER RELATIONSHIPS IN THE PRINCIPALITY OF WALES: 1282–1415

Relations between the English and the Welsh of the principality of the 14th century were precarious and often punitive; however, as the relationship was pervasive and lasting, ultimately it was to everyone's advantage, particularly the gentry of the principality, that it worked. This thesis demonstrates the interrelationships, particularly in power structures between the key actors of Crown administration in England with the key actors of the principality, particularly those influenced by the Crown administration beginning with Llywelyn the Last to Owain Glyndŵr and some key players in between, as well as examples of crisis times: the pestilence of the mid-14th century, the rebellion and insurrections of Rhys ap Maredudd, Madog ap Llywelyn, and Owain ap Thomas ap Rhodri, who at least temporarily had the backing of the king of France, thus making his claim to regain his lands an international issue. Infused in part by these actions and helped along by the bards, poets, and other discontented elites, the Glyndŵr Rebellion ushered in the 15th century, which led to the Punitive Acts of 1401–1402 and a restriction against claims for "Injuries Sustained in the Late Rebellion"[31] in 1413. The principality might have been completely crushed, particularly after the Glyndŵr Rebellion, but it survived and developed into the beginning of a modern nation to continue its uneasy process of coexistence and synthesis.[32]

By 1415 in the principalities of North and South Wales, the population distribution, settlement patterns, forms of agriculture, networks of towns, lines of trade, and distribution of wealth and power had changed significantly. The Crown's Welsh possessions had metamorphed from their 11th-century medieval models closer to their 17th-century early modern ones.[33] Regarding George Vold's assertion that people in opposition to dominant groups are the ones who are most likely to break the law,[34] we have some prominent examples in Llywelyn ap Gruffudd, Rhys ap Maredudd, Owain ap Thomas ap Rhodri, and, unavoidably, Owain Glyndŵr. Glyndŵr is particularly significant to this study as his rebellion, which was overwhelming for its scope and the potential for change, reflected the wishes and ambitions of the gentry and elite from the Welsh nobility, to the clergy, prophets, and poets, even beyond Wales to the anti-pope. This was the time of the Great Schism in the Catholic Church and there were two distinct parts. One was based in Rome, Italy, the other in Avignon, France. Each had its own pope.

When it is considered that the population of Wales was an undetermined fraction of that of England, and that Welsh wealth and influence were negligible, and that the rebellion caused profound damage to the economies of all areas of Wales, the duration of the rebellion and tenacity of its supporters are somewhat surprising. Those factors indicate the degree to which the Welsh elite wanted liberation, believed the prophecies and sought personal advantage, enhancing their Welsh group identity to an embryonic form of nationalism.

The crisis of the Black Death played its macabre role in shaping society in the mid-14th century, not only in the principalities, of course, but throughout Europe. The pestilence played a large part in reshaping economies and changing the perspectives and expectations of the survivors. As they had lived through a horrific, unpredictable crisis (or crises, for those who were exposed to more than one infestation), they had an economy to rebuild and somewhat greater liberty with which to lead their lives, as the societal structures were loosened and a feeling of tentativeness entered daily life reflected in contracts and tenant agreements.[35] As stated, the principality lost as much as half its population,[36] a problem compounded by women giving birth to fewer children during the times of the epidemics of 1348–1349, the 1350s, and 1361–1369. As cattle were affected as well, the economic devastation of the Black Death lasted well into the 1390s.

I have tried to reveal links between prophecy, church, and clergy in their use as tools of power, politics, and propaganda, especially as they influenced and supported one another. The church of the 14th century was itself facing its own schism with its crisis and rebellion, as well as significant structural change, as in the abridgement of the Roman pope's power and the social differences between the upper and lower clergy. Ultimately, the relationship between prophecy, church, and clergy was one of power politics as well as of faith.

As mentioned earlier, the Roman pope was head of a split faction of Christendom of the time; the alternative pope the alternative head of the church, and in those roles they dealt with their hierarchies. In those roles as well the pope of Rome and anti-pope in Avignon dealt with English kings and, at the turn of the 15th century, the king's struggling alternative leader in Wales, Owain Glyndŵr. As Welsh bards supported Glyndŵr, so did many of the clergy of Wales.[37] They, in turn, preached messages from their pulpits that echoed the messages of the bards to weave sympathy and gather support for Glyndŵr.

Certainly there were issues between Welsh people and the Welshmen who undertook offices in the principality for the English, owing to the nature of the administrators' work and the variable honesty of the officers. Group identity issues no doubt were involved regarding to which group, English or Welsh, the officer showed his loyalty; also involved were the possibilities that may have occurred of his profiting at the expense of his Welsh peers, kindred and friends.

Additionally, the enforcers of the Welsh law, the *mechni,* had experienced a decline in power by the 13th century. By the end of that century, English criminal law had a uniformity that the Welsh criminal law lacked.[38] Edward's establishment of the system of courts revolutionized legal procedure in the principality for criminal cases.[39] The courts were "the most important institutional innovation in local government,"[40] particularly as the king expected the men of the shire to gather at the county court to hear and be judged by the Crown's law.[41]

The future Edward IV began policies to provide administrative inclusion with the English for Welsh people in the principality. These policies included calls to parliament.[42] In this way it seems that he won some Welsh loyalty. It is easy to surmise that his actions were defensive to a degree, to forestall or prevent uprisings.[43]

Ultimately, the cooperation of the *uchelwyr* (gentry) is not surprising. The *uchelwyr* were obliged to carve roles for themselves as they were interrelated between the English and Welsh. On a more cynical note, the cooperation of well-placed and rewarded insiders has been essential in every occupation in history, and the gentry of the principalities of North and South Wales were in positions to play that role. They played their roles in service to their homes in Wales, which they loved and doubtless wanted to protect, including political practices, such as the rendering of petitions after annexation that accounted for the movement from bad to better that is a component of group conflict.[44] To cite Boulding, again, however, and relate his philosophies to the principality of the 14th century:[45] all was not conflict and warfare, and to a significant degree the Welsh and English in the principality developed cooperative ways of life to enable them to live without frequent royal intervention or violent conflict.

Realistically, greater power and influence were possible to the gentry through cooperation with and adaptation to English institutions, and many of the *uchelwyr* assumed similar roles to those their ancestors had played for other conquerors. The roles ought not to be seen as traitorous to Wales as both the English and Welsh of this period were adapting to, changing, and being influenced by institutions that were themselves adapting to the principality of the 14th century.

Now to shift focus from an analysis of situations in the 14th century to the peril of the documents that describe them. The following contains excerpts from a letter by two retired professors to dispute the sale of a collection of historic manuscripts from an academic library. This is another example of building an argument by presenting facts. It is structured similarly to many other essays in this book: introductory paragraph, first supporting argument, second supporting argument, additional points made in the third and fourth paragraphs, and a conclusion.

Unlike a historical essay, which is a combination of facts, opinions, time filters, and analysis, this letter to the *Western Mail*, Wales' national newspaper, is a reaction to a proposed action. The authors are anticipating future events and are trying to stop them.

LIBRARY: EMERITI EXPRESS DEEP CONCERN

SIR—The reports in the Western Mail (September 3) of the decision to sell a part of Cardiff Library's collection of valuable early volumes, among them some of specific interest to Wales in the fields of historiography, cartography, topography and literature, is a matter of deep concern and dismay.

It is inconceivable that the capital city's historic library should take such a course of action—in a city that is home to a renowned university that boasts a Nobel scholar, a major university teaching hospital, and a national museum; a city that not long ago sought the title of European City of Culture.

One cannot imagine a major library institution in Dublin, Edinburgh or London treating such treasures in its collections as disposable assets.

Clearly the people who took the decision to take this course of action are fully aware of the market price of the volumes but, alas, they seem to know little of their value.

They also seem to be unaware that their role is surely that of careful custodians of the collection and not irresponsible owners.

We, the undersigned, urge the executive committee of Cardiff council to take immediate steps to prevent this action which so impoverishes our capital and country's cultural assets and so demeans the status of its major library institution.[46]

A LETTER REQUESTING AN APPEAL

Following is a fictional letter appealing the dean of graduate students to reconsider a cross-disciplinary dissertation:

Dear Mr. Goetz,

This letter is to request an appeal of the decision reached about my Ph.D. dissertation, *For Whom the Cat Meows*. I contend that the examiners had not read the dissertation, therefore, could not evaluate its content.

The late Dr. Feline Fancier used diagrams of cats' meows to assess situations of conflict and cooperation that were identified by the sociologist, Professor Nuff Bulletz. Many of the meow diagrams, which demonstrated a range from "extremely frustrated" to "content, but spoiled," including Dr. Fancier's model of a cat that had been petted for five consecutive hours, have been consulted as a significant part of the research for this dissertation.

There were ongoing arguments using conflict theory within the thesis, as well as footnotes and bibliographic references. The examiners did not use effective follow-up questions regarding feline conflict theory.

Again, citing these reasons, I request that this dissertation be reassessed for its evaluation of and contribution to the field.

Points of contention regarding the examiners' assessments:

Part of the internal examiner's critique was that "much of the material does not relate to feline conflict, but to cooperation and synthesis, the references to 'conflict theory' are only sporadic, so that the argument as a whole appears to be fragmented and unsystematic" Feline conflict theory, as it is called later in the examiners' assessment, particularly that of the late Dr. Bulletz, is used to assess and critique conditions of cooperation and synthesis for cats.

The examiners inaccurately stated that I did not think I needed further supervision. I had changed the structure of the supervision to consult my adviser, Professor Buck Brown, when I thought it was necessary. Professor Brown contributed information and suggested source material during the revision.

I was encouraged throughout by my adviser, Professor Brown. Professor Bulletz's theories were applied by Bulletz back to 16th-century Europe, because they required relatively sophisticated societies that had the time and money to indulge their cats' petting needs. Professor Bulletz's historical analysis involved the beginning of colonization and empire. Because the nature of conflict and cooperation increased in cats with secure homes who simultaneously felt the need to defend their property and the desire to indulge their love of being petted, the theories developed by Dr. Fancier, the late Peter Dogmatic, and others as described in the dissertation, held up under this examination. This thesis, however, was not meant to compare the situations described in cats and kittens to the general behavior of all mammals. There are, however, many references utilized of the sources of petting climates and behavior.

I was appalled by the number of errors and omissions made by the examiners in the assessment and the subsequent explanation by professors Smith and Wesson. I would not accept this degree of error in any assessment of any research format that I have used to date, and I do not accept it as a proper evaluation of the dissertation.

The more responsible a profession purports to be, the more accountable its members are obliged to be.

Sincerely,
Lindsay Craig

AN APPEAL TO THE EMOTIONS

One important element of persuasive writing is an appeal to the emotions. Stories of animals in distress whose situations change spark emotions similar to those aroused by stories of children under duress. It is important to tell these stories in ways that are palatable to readers and audiences to increase their identification with the subject and willingness to read the entire story.

Following is an example of a story of a dual rescue: feline and human. It is a story that includes examples of persuasion. Look at the examples that influence me and, through me, the readers. Notice that the beginning paragraph summarizes the lesson of the story.

THE MISSY CHRONICLE

Missy is in her accustomed spot as I write: only inches from me, her back paws against my laptop, her front paws and face in a relaxed, settled-for-sleep posture. At nine years and six months, the little forest cat, who seems to have some Maine coon traits, has changed homes and service people at least three times—I give a hollow laugh whenever people are called cats' "owners." Missy has survived a major move from Flagstaff, Arizona, to Rhode Island and bullying from a larger, territorial cat. Missy is assertive, dignified, playful, and sweet, and in April 2008 we celebrated our first anniversary. We have a lot in common, including our sharing the importance of rescue and being valued.

In April 2007, I was a recent replant to Providence from Cardiff, Wales. I was between jobs, and the one thing I knew was that I didn't want to stay in Providence. In the previous 10 years, I had lived and worked abroad in the capacities of librarian and Peace Corps volunteer in Jamaica and history researcher and writer in the United Kingdom. Cats had been part of my life since childhood, and my brother suggested that I might get one in Providence. I planned to move again, however. "I wouldn't know if I could find another home for one," I had protested.

One of my friends was connected to an animal rescue network in Rhode Island and had hosted a cable television program called "Pet Talk." She and her husband came for dinner in early April, and as they were leaving, I experienced an overwhelming feeling of needing a cat.

"Maxine," I said suddenly. "Do you know of any cat who needs a home?"

"I can check," Maxine offered.

A few days later I received a follow-up call from Maxine. A friend of hers knew of a couple of cats Maxine was fairly certain were Maine coons; one of them eight years old and the other one six, and they needed homes. I called Maxine's friend Carol and was told that the six-year-old had been adopted, but the eight-year-old was still available, as far as she knew. Carol put the eight-year-old's person and me in touch with each other, and after some phone tag, we talked. I was a little nervous about adopting another cat; it had been eight years since my last two, but this one was living in one room of a house. She needed a new home quickly, because she was fending off a 20-pound feline bully. Giving myself a week to make arrangements, I ordered a luxurious litter box and began reading up on Maine coons. I remember particularly some advice from many online articles, which said a Maine coon could be a friend but would stay independent.

"Ah, that will work well if she needs to be rehoused," I thought, with the ruthless assurance of one who had not yet met her next furry charge.

The day came for Missy's relocation. The litter box had arrived a few days before in a huge box that I calculated could be Missy's room for quiet time within the apartment. The cardboard box made the bigger hit with the little feline, for her own litter box came with her to her new home, and she had no need of the luxury one. The first half hour went smoothly: we set up Missy's old litter box and her food and water dishes, and her service person emerita let me in on two of my new companion's less attractive habits: "She walks on computer keyboards and tears up paper." To my mind a writer has to deal with enough critics without your own roommate mutilating your prose, but I said, "She does?" in a fairly croaky way, and was quiet.

"And she'll lie across your throat," came as another ironic honorable mention, because when not writing or editing, I sometimes give presentations and speeches. The knowledge that Missy was going to impede all of my paid activities and that I didn't care says something, be it positive or negative, about love.

"Oh, eh," I replied. "Perhaps we should have a two-week trial period." Truly, though, my caveat about the trial period was in case Missy shouldn't like me, which had happened with another cat, whose human sibling was a—gulp!—literary agent.

Missy was pretty miserable during her transition. For 16 days she alternately hid, vomited, and begged to go home—particularly at 8 P.M.— when, I surmised, the family had probably gathered with the pets to watch television, for Missy would get onto my bed, which is across from the TV, and look at the blank screen significantly. Our first real breakthrough came from her fascination with a small straw owl my brother had given me, which was hanging from a loop on my printer. She began fondling the owl, meowing, and looking toward the door of the apartment, where Missy's scratching fish, a combination toy and nail file, was hanging.

"Do you want this to be over your scratching fish?" I asked, and to my modest amazement the little cat began walking toward the door, meowing as she went. I followed with the owl and looped it over the door handle, while Missy purred and began happily to play with it. To my gratification, she didn't demolish the straw ornament, but continued gently to fondle it.

Other breakthroughs followed. A day or two after that, I awoke to Missy's lying on my chest and kneading me with standard feline nursing motions. After that, she did try to lie on my throat, but I dissuaded her, reminding her that the more that I was able to work, the more toys there would be for her. We had a major altercation the day Missy's feline footwork-from-Hell erased an entire page of a speech that I was preparing, but I realized I would have to save my work every couple of sentences.

Missy gave me a major clue to her instincts one night when I raised my arm to lift my back scratcher and she shook and ran under the bed. I followed, and when she emerged I petted her and said, "Missy, I promise I will never hurt you. You are safe here and no one will bother you." I picked her up and continued cuddling and crooning while she purred. To that time her back legs had been stiff, and I had assumed she had arthritis. At times, standing and walking were painful for her, and she sometimes missed her goal when she jumped. Wonderfully, after our major cuddle session her legs began to relax, and her standing, walking, and jumping became easier and more successful. I mentioned this rehabilitation to Carol. "She was tense," Carol concurred.

In February, when Missy and I had been living together nearly 10 months, I gave a dinner party for a group of women who all had rescued animals. Maxine was one of the guests, and we began talking about her experiences in a particular rescue network. I asked her what her most satisfying rescue had been. She gave a broad smile.

"You and Missy are the most successful," she replied.

Lest the preceding be dismissed as only a cat story written by a devoted pet owner, the story fits into this chapter because it is full of persuasive paragraphs, but the only vocal persuading that Missy engages in is purring (the hiding, vomiting, cuddling, and so on are excluded as not vocal.) During the story, I realize after some initial struggling with inter-species behavior and communication, that each is more therapeutic for the other than at first thought. This realization is brought home at the end, when I am included in Maxine's naming the most successful rescue.

NOTES

Louis D. Brandeis, *Brainy Quote*, "Louis D. Brandeis Quotes," www.brainyquote.com/quotes/authors/l/louis_d_brandeis.html.

1. R. M. Ritter, *The Oxford Style Manual* (New York: Oxford University Press, 2003); R. M. Ritter, *The Oxford Guide to Style* (New York: Oxford University Press, 2002).

2. William Kelleher Storey, *Writing History: A Guide for Students* (New York: Oxford University Press, 2004), 107–111.

3. John Burton, *Conflict: Human Needs Theory* (New York: Palgrave Macmillan, 1993).

4. Kenneth E. Boulding, *Three Faces of Power* (Newbury Park, CA: Sage Publications, Inc, 1989), 44.

5. Ibid., 160.

6. Ibid., 173.

7. Ibid., 175–177.

8. Harry Kreisler, "National Security Through Stable Peace: Conversation with Kenneth Boulding, University Professor Emeritus of Economics, University of Colorado," March 16, 1987, Conversations with History: Institute of International Studies, University of California at Berkeley, globetrotter.berkeley.edu/conversations/Boulding/kboulding con2.html.

9. Kenneth E. Boulding, *Conflict and Defense: A General Theory* (New York: Harper and Row, 1970), 280.

10. George Vold, T. J. Bernard, and J. B. Snipes, *Conflict Criminology* (Oxford: Oxford University Press 1998); Richard Quinney, *The Social Reality of Crime* (Boston: Little Brown & Co. 1970).

11. Vincent Wilson Jr. and Gale S. McClung, *The Book of Distinguished American Women: New Revised Edition* (Brookeville, MD: American History Research Associates, 2003), 48.

12. Ibid.

13. Ibid.

14. Carolyn Davis, "ADA and Libraries," presentation to the Warwick Public Library, Warwick, Rhode Island, April 28, 2009.

15. A. Lupack and B.T. Lupack, eds., "The Camelot Project," The University of Rochester, www.lib.rochester.edu/camelot/cphome.stm.

16. B. Taithe and T. Thornton, *Prophecy: The Power of Inspired Language in History, 1300–2000* (Stroud, UK: Gloucestershire, 1997), 18.

17. G. Ashe, ed., *The Quest for Arthur's Britain* (Aylesbury, UK: Praeger Publishers, 1968).

18. Ibid., 4–5.

19. Ibid., 5.

20. J. Gillingham, *The English in the Twelfth Century: Imperialism, National Identity and Political Values* (Suffolk, UK: Boydell Press, 2000), xxii.

21. Ibid., 20–22.

22. G. Ashe, *The Quest for Arthur's Britain*, 6.

23. J. Gillingham, *The English in the Twelfth Century*, 22.

24. Ibid., 20–21.

25. Ibid., 21.

26. David Carpenter, *The Struggle for Mastery: The Penguin History of Britain 1066–1284* (London: Penguin, 2005), 188.

27. The National Library of Wales, Aberystwyth, "Treasures: The Black Book of Carmarthen," www.llgc.org.uk/index.php?id=digitalmirror.

28. PBS, "Wounded Knee," *We Shall Remain*. A Production of American Experience in Association with NAPT, www.pbs.org/wgbh/amex/weshallremain/, p. 24.

29. William Kelleher Storey, *Writing History: A Guide for Students*, 62–65.

30. Ibid., 63–64.

31. Ivor Bowen, ed., *The Statues of Wales* (London: T.F. Unwin, 1908), 37.

32. Sir Robert Rees Davies, *Conquest, Coexistence and Change: Wales 1063–1415* (Oxford: Oxford University Press, 1987), 463.

33. Ibid.

34. Tom O'Connor, *Conflict Criminology*, www.apsu.edu/oconnort/crim/crimtheory15.htm.

35. William Rees, *The Black Death in England and Wales as Exhibited in Manorial Documents* (London: The Royal Society of Medicine, 1923), 17.

36. Bertha H. Putnam, *The Enforcement of the Statutes of Labourers during the First Decade after the Black Death: 1349–1359* (New York: Columbia University 1908), 1.

37. Glanmor Williams, *The Welsh Church from Conquest to Reformation* (Cardiff, Wales: University of Wales Press, 1962), 218–222.

38. Sir J. E. Lloyd, *Owain Glendower* (London: Llanarch Press, 1966), xxx–xxxi.

39. William Henry Waters, *The Edwardian Settlement of North Wales in its Administrative and Legal Aspects:1284–1343* (Westport, CT: Greenwood Press), 99.

40. Ibid.

41. Ibid.

42. A. D. Carr, *Owen of Wales: The End of the House of Gwynedd* (Cardiff: University of Wales, 1991), 72.

43. Ibid.

44. K. E. Boulding, *Conflict and Defense: A General Theory* (New York: University Press of America), 249.

45. K. E. Boulding, *Three Faces of Power* (New York: Sage Publications), 223.

46. *Archivalia*, "Cardiff Library: Emeriti express deep concern," archiv.twoday.net/stories/5207108/.

CHAPTER 3

Problems and Solutions

I am grateful for all my problems. After each one was overcome, I became stronger and more able to meet those that were still to come. I
grew in all my difficulties.

—James Cash Penney

Identify your problems, but give your power and energy to solutions.
—Anthony Robbins

It is a common experience that a problem difficult at night is resolved
in the morning after the committee of sleep has worked on it.
—John Steinbeck

THE BASIC DON'TS OF ALL WRITING

Plagiarism

The problem of plagiarism goes beyond poor writing into the realm of
crime, and it can be difficult to disprove. In her book *A Manual for Writers
of Research Papers, Dissertations and Theses*, Kate Turabian lists some examples of inadvertent plagiarism. These examples are not uncommon to students, but all writers are vulnerable.

> You cited a source but used its exact words without putting them in a para-
> graph or a block quotation.
> You paraphrased a source and cited it, but in words so similar to those of
> your source that they are almost a quotation. . . .
> You used ideas or methods from a source but failed to cite it.[1]

Turabian also warns against "inappropriate assistance" in the editing of and suggestions for a paper or dissertation. For either, proofreading is acceptable; rewriting is not.[2] Extensive editing and rewriting frequently occur prior to an article's or book's publication, but extensive editing by anyone other than the author is not appropriate for an essay, a thesis, or a dissertation that is to be submitted for a grade.

On the topic of acknowledging help in a class paper or thesis, Turabian states:

> For a class paper, you usually aren't required to acknowledge general criticism, minor editing, or help from a school writing tutor, but you must acknowledge help that's special or extensive. Your instructor sets the rules, so ask.
>
> For a thesis, dissertation, or published work, you're not required to acknowledge routine help, though it's courteous and often politic to do so in a preface. . . . But you must acknowledge special or extensive editing and cite in a note major ideas or phrases provided by others.[3]

The amount of help that an essay writer may accept can be difficult to gage. Proofreading, for example, consists principally of correction, not editing. It is the proofreader's job to see that the sentences are complete and correctly spelled and spaced, that the punctuation is accurate, and that the document is correctly aligned.[4] A proofreader who makes many suggestions or changes in the text is editing, which the author may or may not welcome. The following is a short list of basic "don't"s and corrections:

GRAMMAR AND SPELLING

Incorrect:

Me and the boys cancelled our trip due to bad whether.

Correct:

The boys and I cancelled our trip because the weather was bad.

PUNCTUATION

Good punctuation makes sentences and paragraphs clear. Be sure to use punctuation marks correctly.

A period (.) ends a sentence. A comma (,) pauses a sentence. Among other things, it is used for a list of items (bread, apples, and cheese), or the beginning of a quote (Sasha said, "Ali has brown hair.").

Incorrect:

Don't fall in love with semi-colons; make sentences clear; make sentences concise—don't use a dash when you need a period.

Correct:

Don't fall in love with semi-colons. Write sentences that are clear and concise. Don't use a dash when you need a period.

SENTENCE FRAGMENTS

Good writing consists of sentences that express thoughts and actions clearly, completely, and concisely. Sentence fragments are parts of sentences that convey the meaning of a full sentence without the formal structure.

Sentence: Did you eat yet?
Fragment: Eat yet?

RUN-ON SENTENCES AND PARAGRAPHS

Sentences express complete thoughts and actions. Paragraphs express complete subjects. Some clues to whether a sentence or paragraph is written well are the excessive use of "and"s, "but"s, or punctuation to hold it together. When in doubt, break it down.

Run-on Sentence: I woke up, got dressed, ate breakfast, and walked to the gym for a workout where I saw my friend Tom and we worked out together.
Corrected Sentences: I woke up, got dressed, ate breakfast, and walked to the gym for a workout. There I saw my friend Tom, and we worked out together

Run-on paragraph: Whenever she passed a chicory plant and really noticed it, our mother would say, "Chicory," and touch it gently. Sometimes she would add, "I love chicory." The gentle ceremony influenced me in a way that I didn't connect when really young: when I received my first cat and really appreciated her, I would stroke her tiger-striped fur and say, "Andy. I love Andy." Although not intentionally copying Mom, I was playing a part in relaying a message that is important and not emphasized enough. Gentle expressions and rituals of love are important. If made a part of a person's life, they can begin a chain that can have further-reaching effects than we know.
Repaired paragraphs: Whenever she passed a chicory plant and really noticed it, our mother would say, "Chicory," and touch it gently. Sometimes

she would add, "I love chicory." The gentle ceremony influenced me in a way that I didn't connect when really young: when I received my first cat and really appreciated her, I would stroke her tiger-striped fur and say, "Andy. I love Andy."

Although not intentionally copying Mom, I was playing a part in relaying a message that is important and not emphasized enough. Gentle expressions and rituals of love are important. If made a part of a person's life, they can begin a chain that can have further-reaching effects than we know.

The corrected paragraphs demonstrate the different subjects of the ritual and its interpretation.

INAPPROPRIATE USE OF PRONOUNS

To begin a sentence with a pronoun instead of a defined name is bad practice in speaking or writing. The subjects of written and spoken sentences need to be defined for the readers or an audience.

Subject unnamed:

We sent her the information, but have not received a reply.

Subject named:

Amara and I sent Annette the information, but have not received a reply.

Effective Letters

Following is a fictitious letter of reference for an assistant project coordinator who specializes in conflict resolution.

The letter is an example of persuasive writing. There is a point of view, background, description, supporting statements of fact and opinion, and a conclusion that follows logically from the supporting statements.

Dear Poached Egg Coordinator,

As the coordinator of the Scrambled Eggs Restaurant chain, I supervised Mary Mellow for two years. Ms. Mellow served as the assistant project coordinator for the Scrambled Eggs Project from April 1, 2003, to April 1, 2005, and she created omelets and egg creams.

The first paragraph introduces the writer and his or her relationship to Ms. Mellow. The following paragraphs provide examples of Ms. Mellow's fine work, and the letter ends with a recommendation. The letter's structure is similar to the five-paragraph essay, but is shorter.

In her role as professional omelet maker, Ms. Mellow assisted Scrambled Eggs in making hundreds of omelets and egg creams. Ms. Mellow collaborated with Dr. Rose Havarti to coordinate the development of a national Scrambled Eggs outlet. The national outlet serves a network of egg lovers breakfast and brunch specialties.

Ms. Mellow faced many challenges in developing the outlet, which she met with tenacity and fortitude. Ms. Mellow coordinated mediation sessions for franchise owners to work out their issues and developed constructive ways to deal with the multitude of challenges inherent in developing a national restaurant chain. A resource center for franchise owners was one of her major contributions.

I give Ms. Mellow the highest possible recommendation.

Following is a fictitious letter (the book titles and authors listed are real) concerning the review of a manuscript. The author of the letter begins with an acknowledgment of the assessment and praises its fairness. Next, she mentions specific topics about which the reviewers have misused a significant phrase. The letter is cordial, but on point.

Jane Inkstain
Executive Editor
Anytown Press

Dear Ms. Inkstain,

I received the associate editor's assessment of my manuscript, *Conflict Theory Applied to Medieval Times Can Be Fun*. I was impressed by the quality overall; however, I should like to bring your attention to certain important discrepancies:

Control Theory: I accept the statement in the letter of October 11, 2008, that the reviewers' statement of "control theory" instead of "conflict theory" was "a simple error in the composition of the assessment"; however, I should like to point out that it was potentially a significant error, as it refers to specific work in at least three other fields. Control theory is used in sociology (as is conflict theory; in fact, a form of conflict control is defined in Kenneth Boulding's *Conflict and Defense: A General Theory*. The book was used as a source for the manuscript. In different contexts, control theory is also used in engineering and mathematics, for example, F. L. Lewis, *Applied Optimal Control and Estimation* and Eduardo D. Sontag, *Mathematical Control Theory: Deterministic Finite Dimensional Systems*, 2nd ed.

The late Kenneth E. Boulding used diagrams of situations of conflict and cooperation to assess conditions of peace, cooperativeness, and conflict to assess societies at various stages of peace, cooperation, conflict, and war. Some of these situations have been applied to the thesis. The late George Vold and Richard Quinney, whose works are also referred to and evaluated regarding my manuscript, were and are specialists in the situations that constitute crime, the groups that are in a position to define crime, and those that are defined as having committed crimes. Their works are referred to repeatedly in the manuscript regarding the situations of conflict and crime between the medieval Welsh and English—the Punitive Acts, for example—and were explained in the manuscript. The work contains ongoing arguments using conflict theory and footnotes and bibliographic references.

Thank you for your attention to these significant points.

Sincerely

HOSTILE OR APATHETIC AUDIENCES

Situations with nonreceptive audiences are more likely in professional forums than with students' essays, but strategies to deal with hostile or apathetic readers are beneficial for everyone. Here are some examples of situations in which your audience may be less than receptive and some strategies to help you deal with the situations.

1. You are writing about the need to increase funding for public education, and your readers include one group that has just been laid off and another group that sends its children to private or parochial schools.
2. You are writing for an audience of small business owners about the need to increase physical access to their buildings.

Persuasion is most effective when writers understand the perspectives of their audience, and acknowledge those perspectives respectfully. What are the concerns of an unsympathetic audience; what actually are the reasons for an audience's difficulties with a particular proposal? For you truly to know the reasons, you need to become familiar with the facts—avoid conventional wisdom, assumptions, projections, and the like, and do some significant fact-finding. What are the real situations and issues, and how can you become knowledgeable about them?

In the first example, it would help to read something about the options private, parochial, and charter schools offer. What qualities do the public schools offer that are attractive and might compete with or differ from the others? Also, what incentives might you find and offer to address the concerns of those who are unemployed?

In the second example, how might you demonstrate that enabling people who are disabled to have access to their business benefits proprietors (besides reminding them that it is the law of the land, which they probably know)? You need to conduct research or access existing current research.

TALK TO PEOPLE

The best way to find out what your readers are thinking is to talk to them. This is particularly feasible if you are based in the same geographic area in which your publication will appear or in which you will make your presentation, but low-cost telephoning, teleconferencing, and e-mail make this approach feasible wherever you and your readers are.

One example is a presentation I gave about the development of the Jamaica Coalition on Disability, the need for which was made apparent by a national survey of disability-services agency directors and employees. The survey results pointed to the need for cooperation instead of competition among agencies. After seven months of meetings, the agency directors were convinced that a coalition would truly be beneficial to their agencies and clients. The research persuaded them.[5]

Eleanor Roosevelt is a historically famous example of the benefits of finding out what people are thinking and doing. At the insistence of Louis Howe, Franklin Roosevelt's campaign manager, Mrs. Roosevelt became the newly disabled Mr. Roosevelt's "legs" in the early 1920s. She and Howe traveled all over New York, and later the United States, to keep Roosevelt apprised of current events. The results of those early efforts contributed to Roosevelt's election as governor of New York and, ultimately, as president of the United States.

You say you don't have a spouse and a campaign manager who are willing to go on fact-finding trips for you? All the better. Look at how much time you have to prepare, and go yourself. At any stage from high school to professional, your readers will know and appreciate that you have done your homework.

Training sessions to teach speakers to deal with hostile groups in America go back at least to the 1830s. The slavery abolitionist Theodore Weld gave abolitionist sisters Angelina and Sarah Grimké instructions on how to deal with hostile audiences before they began a lecture tour in the eastern United States.[6] At that time, audiences had issues not only with the sisters' abolitionist perspectives but also with their gender and their speaking in public.[7] The sisters continued to speak in public to audiences that were willing to listen, and this established a certain level of acceptance in more than one arena.[8]

Addressing mixed audiences produced a more fundamental challenge—a woman's *right* to do so. . . . Angelina responded [to the sisters' critics], 'We have given great offense. . . . We are willing to bear the brunt [of criticism], if we can [eliminate the barriers] which [lie] in the way of women's rights, true dignity, honor and usefulness.[9]

Angelina wrote *Appeal to the Christian Women of the South* (1836), to encourage southern women to join the abolitionist movement for the sake of white couples' marriages and for the benefit of the slaves.[10] The discussion of white men who father the children of women who were enslaved was highly controversial. Sarah published *Epistle to the Clergy of the Southern States* in 1836.[11] Angelina published *Appeal to the Women of the Nominally Free States* in 1837, around the time they began a lecture tour of Congregational churches in the northeast United States.[12]

Angelina and Sarah Grimké continued to be strong advocates for women's rights while advocating for the end of slavery and discrimination against races. That was a considerable amount of persuasive writing and speaking to undertake, and the hostility ultimately helped their cause.[13]

The Grimké sisters were able to generate and sustain audiences' and readers' interests, thus increasing attention and promoting discussion about them and their topics. The abilities to get people to attend presentations, buy books, and talk about the writers, presenters, and their topics are significant achievements in persuasion that all persuasive writers and speakers may employ.

Now let us move to another method of fact-finding: asking questions.

Questions

Lane and Bernabei suggest that a creative way to deal with a topic is to focus on the questions it raises:

A question is like this beam of light. It points in a particular direction and illuminates certain parts of the argument when you try to answer it. Finding the right question to begin with can help you organize your essay by showing you which details to include and which to leave out. Questions also help to illuminate all the angles.

For example, here is a list of questions about a school uniform issue. Try answering them and you will develop a point of view on the topic. . . .

Do you hate school uniforms?
What will school uniforms do to a sense of children's individuality?
When in history and in what countries are school uniforms standard?

Who stands to benefit from school uniforms?
Why is the question of school uniforms an important issue?
If teachers wore uniforms, how would it affect the school?
Which of those questions show the most your point of view?
Which question brought out the least information?[14]

Questions are mental exercises that enable people to think about different aspects of a topic. To be an able questioner is to train yourself to think about different points of view and to probe issues effectively. The author and humorist James Thurber wrote, "It is better to know some of the questions than all of the answers."[15] Asking appropriate questions adds to and exercises people's wisdom and enables them to appreciate the scope of your knowledge or probing of an issue. Asking questions in verbal or written form increases the audience's or readers' interest and participation in your discussion as well as the likelihood of your audience's discussing a valid point that hasn't occurred to you. In short, questions in constructive forms are stimulating for the presenter or author and for those in the roles of receivers.

USE FEEDBACK BEFORE AND AFTER COMPLETION

Alongside talking to people is its even more important mate, listening to people (or interpreting your research). What are your findings telling you? Allow yourself to be open to persuasion as you, in turn, attempt to persuade. The result will be a more detailed and layered report that will be a better vehicle of persuasion.

Then comes the time when your essay is handed in and graded, the presentation made, or the report published. What does your postdelivery feedback tell you about the job you did? Take it all in and learn from it. Pay particular attention to feedback that is negative but on point. (Disregard the abusive and off-target stuff.) Useful feedback, pro and con, will teach you some significant lessons that you can apply to your next project.

PASSION/ARROGANCE: ANTICIPATE AND ACCEPT DISAGREEMENT, AND DEAL WITH IT WITHIN YOUR WRITING

All right, you are passionate about your subject. You have been researching it for anywhere from two weeks to 30 years plus, and you and the subject are entwined. You are truly an authority, and the world should acknowledge your expertise and accept what you say without question. Well, prepare to justify yourself further. High levels of acceptance and approval occur sometimes but should not be counted on. You will have to prove your abilities repeatedly, whether you are a student learning to put together a research project or a 35-year veteran of dozens of projects.

> Real opinions lie deep within all of us, but gaining access to them can sometimes be a complex and harrowing process. Outrageous opinions, however, grow on the surface like fungus and daytime TV talk shows. It has been said that America is held together by a tapestry of outrageous opinions. Actually, it hasn't been said till now, and that's how you feel when you have strong opinions: like your view of the world is unique and important.[16]

Yes, indeed, to Barry Lane's and Gretchen Bernabei's wisdom. Whether the opinions are real, outrageous, or both, part of the art of persuasion lies in knowing that everyone has opinions and frequently those opinions differ from the presenter's, and the presenter should work with that knowledge appropriately.

The writer who expects only acceptance and praise for an essay, article, presentation, or book that states a position unequivocally is someone who will soon head for a fall. Passions, education, and experiences do not preclude others' corresponding and alternating or opposing passions, education, and experience, and an experienced persuasive writer accommodates these. It all refers to your familiarity with your audience and your abilities to present your points while acknowledging that your readers' situations and needs may differ from yours. Remember, the goal is to recruit and maintain their respect and possible alliances while explaining to them in cogent ways why your points are valid. The writer or presenter might cite examples from the audience's own experiences. Following are two short examples; the first is a true give-and-take that occurred in a college classroom many years ago among a college freshman, a teaching assistant who was a native of France, and another freshman in the class.

> First freshman to the teaching assistant: "What school did you learn English at?"
> Second freshman to the first: "What school did *you* learn English at?"

When you are trying to determine someone's credentials for a professional setting, it helps to demonstrate that you, yourself, know the basics.

The second example developed from a lengthy but fact-challenged so-
liloquy that a woman named Jane delivered to express her opposition to
a variety of social legislation geared to increasing opportunities for education and employment to people who were members of particular minority
groups. Jane's friend Leslie was a member of one. After 15 minutes of listening to the harangue, another woman said simply, "Jane, if there had
been no social legislation in the past hundred years, you would be Leslie's
maid." The point was made and no blood was drawn.

A gentler example and its follow-up are shown in two e-mail messages.

> At times I think that one of the problems that Americans have is not the use
> of freedom of speech, but its interpretation: a perceived corollary of freedom
> of bullying. Individuals and groups are in the habit not just of stating views,
> but stating them repeatedly, venomously, and with the expectation that the
> rest of the community, classroom, state, country, and world must agree. To
> disagree (which is a constitutional right), can mean harm or destruction.
>
> My opinion is that there is a distinction between the right to state an
> opinion and the action of bullying. To enjoy and partake in freedom of
> speech, a person should be willing to tolerate the opinions of others, so, to
> paraphrase, tolerate others as you would wish to be tolerated.[17]

The general response, paraphrased as follows, echoed the need for more
tolerance.

> The death of civility that stems from consideration in human relations is
> disturbing. The hypocrisy of hatred and violence from certain groups would
> be humorous if it were not so real and frightening. Too bad that we cannot
> give the gift of tolerance to those who need it the most!

An arrogant, know-it-all position alienates audiences. As you anticipate
different perspectives and disagreement, your goal is to persuade, not to
bully, and the roads are significantly different. Successful politicians are
true masters of the use of charm and familiarity to promote their agendas.
Tony Blair, the former prime minister of the United Kingdom, who is tremendously in demand as an after-dinner speaker, is an exemplary persuasive writer and speaker. Consider this passage from a speech he made to
the Irish Parliament during a profoundly significant time of transition for
Northern Ireland after the Good Friday Agreement became law in April
1998. The agreement heralded the end of nearly three decades of hostili-
ties between the different political parties and communities in the small

country. The agreement, which was officially recognized on April 10 and 11, 1998, was the culmination of many years of negotiations.

> Members of the Dail and Seanad, after all the long and torn history of our two peoples, standing here as the first British prime minister ever to address the joint Houses of the Oireachtas, I feel profoundly both the history in this event, and I feel profoundly the enormity of the honour that you are bestowing upon me. From the bottom of my heart, *go raibh mile maith agaibh*.[18]

Integrating the native language into the presentation is a constructive action. Audiences appreciate linguistic connections, because bilingual communication not only demonstrates familiarity, but it also takes some effort to integrate appropriately in the context of the presentation. Blair continues:

> Ireland, as you may know, is in my blood. My mother was born in the flat above her grandmother's hardware shop on the main street of Ballyshannon in Donegal. She lived there as a child, started school there and only moved when her father died; her mother remarried and they crossed the water to Glasgow.[19]

Blair introduces a family link, which formed another connection.

> We spent virtually every childhood summer holiday up to when the troubles really took hold in Ireland, usually at Rossnowlagh, the Sands House Hotel, I think it was. And we would travel in the beautiful countryside of Donegal. It was there in the seas off the Irish coast that I learned to swim, there that my father took me to my first pub, a remote little house in the country, for a Guinness, a taste I've never forgotten and which it is always a pleasure to repeat.[20]

Travel around and near Northern Ireland, boyhood swimming, and Blair's first pub experience with his dad are additional nostalgic connections to warm his listeners' hearts!

> Even now, in my constituency of Sedgefield, which at one time had 30 pits or more, all now gone, virtually every community remembers that its roots lie in Irish migration to the mines of Britain.[21]

In the first paragraph Blair complimented his audience; in the next two, he established personal connections to them. Personal touches establish connections and can engender sympathy in the literal sense of "same feeling." All of these are vital when writers or speakers are extending their hands in a peace process, breaking the ice during or after a business acquisition, or otherwise paving the way during a significant transition.

Look at the similar techniques President Obama employed in the following excerpts from his victory speech on November 4, 2008. In that significant time, his speech incorporated celebration and gratitude at a personal level, acknowledged the political and social significance of the election as president of a man who is biracial, and gave thanks for the dedication of the large numbers of people who made it happen.

> It's the answer told by lines that stretched around schools and churches in numbers this nation has never seen; by people who waited three hours and four hours, many for the very first time in their lives, because they believed that this time must be different; that their voices could be that difference.
>
> It's the answer spoken by young and old, rich and poor, Democrat and Republican, black, white, Hispanic, Asian, Native American, gay, straight, disabled and not disabled—Americans who sent a message to the world that we have never been just a collection of individuals or a collection of Red States and Blue States: we are, and always will be, the United States of America.
>
> It's the answer that led those who have been told for so long by so many to be cynical, and fearful, and doubtful of what we can achieve to put their hands on the arc of history and bend it once more toward the hope of a better day.[22]

In this passage, the new president-elect acknowledges the mandate he would have as president, the United States as one whole nation, and the different people who make up that nation. As president of the United States, he acknowledges that he will have many problems to address and will be commander-in-chief to everyone.

> It's been a long time coming, but tonight, because of what we did on this day, in this election, at this defining moment, change has come to America. . . .
>
> I want to thank my partner in this journey, a man who campaigned from his heart and spoke for the men and women he grew up with on the streets of Scranton and rode with on that train home to Delaware, the vice-president-elect of the United States, Joe Biden.
>
> And I would not be standing here tonight without the unyielding support of my best friend for the last 16 years . . . the nation's next first lady, Michelle Obama. Sasha and Malia, . . . you have earned the new puppy that's coming with us to the White House.[23]

Obama acknowledges the societal changes his election signifies. He then identifies the people who worked and sacrificed the most with thumbnail sketches of their backgrounds and their importance to him. He uses truly human touches—and how that puppy made headlines, even during the administration's transition!

> And while she's no longer with us, I know my grandmother is watching, along with the family that made me who I am. I miss them tonight. . . . To my sister Maya, my sister Auma, all my other brothers and sisters—thank you so much for all the support you have given me. I am grateful to them.
>   To my campaign manager David Plouffe,. . . . My chief strategist David Axelrod, . . . and to the best campaign team ever assembled in the history of politics—you made this happen, and I am forever grateful for what you've sacrificed to get it done.[24]

Additional thanks go to his late maternal grandmother, to other family members and the coordinators of the campaign. Obama's rallying cry of "Yes, we can" echo through the paragraphs of his speech that acknowledge his election victory and anticipate victories in the future.

Given these examples, what are some ways to persuade without bullying? They are found in the well being of the writer and presenter, or, to paraphrase, we have met the issues and they are ours.[25]

WHAT FRIGHTENS YOU? CONFRONTING PROFESSIONAL AND PERSONAL DEMONS

Possibly the most challenging types of persuasive essays are those that demand that the writers confront their own issues. Besides dealing with the mechanics of writing and the issues of their readers, how do authors and presenters deal with a situation in which they must present something that is or once was abhorrent to themselves, to an audience? How do writers persuade readers of the importance of the authors' issues?

And more specifically, how do you present an issue in your life, your career, your loved ones' lives, that is neither overdramatized nor underplayed? How do you sustain an objective audience's interest?

Tell the story. Relate the tale as you experienced it. What were your thoughts, feelings, and observations? What was the background of the situation and the larger environment? What has happened since? All of these are effective ways of engaging your readers. An example of this type of autobiographical approach are found in this passage from Elie Wiesel's *Night*:

Man comes closer to God through the questions he asks Him, he liked to say. Therein lies true dialogue. Man asks and God replies. But we don't understand His replies. We cannot understand them. Because they dwell in the depths of our souls and remain there until we die. The real answers, Eliezer, you will find only within yourself.

"And why do you pray, Moishe?" I asked him.

"I pray to the God within me for the strength to ask him the real questions."[26]

And this example from the late Hugh Gallagher's *Blackbird Fly Away: Disabled in an Able-Bodied World* is also effective:

What Roosevelt conceived at Warm Springs seems, on reflection, to be both sensible and obvious, but was, in fact, revolutionary. So far as rehabilitation practice is concerned, Roosevelt grasped certain principles intuitively; his actions and decisions were based upon these principles, even though they had not yet been formalized into words or placed within the context of an organized, philosophical structure. At Warm Springs, Roosevelt and his associates were busy *doing* rehabilitation. As a result, they discovered various principles, and these were later incorporated into a coherent theory of rehabilitation.

This intuitive understanding of a problem and its solution, this development of the principle of the solution in concert with the practical application of the solution, was the method Roosevelt would use later in the New Deal.[27]

Both examples illustrate historical perspectives of the subjects that shaped not only the authors' perspectives but also significant parts of their lives. In the first, Wiesel introduces the reader to part of the beginning of his spiritual quests and his finding a spiritual counselor in the surprising form of an eccentric, Moishe the Beadle, in his hometown, Sighet, in Transylvania. Their meetings provide a backdrop for the extreme challenges to life and faith that the young boy will face. Those challenges have provided decades of questing for the author, whose writings have influenced countless others.

In the second example, Gallagher provides a backdrop developed by Franklin Roosevelt, one of the most influential people personally to deal with poliomyelitis and its after effects. A noted Roosevelt biographer, Gallagher integrates some of his research and perspectives on the founder of Warm Springs, the rehabilitation center in Georgia where Gallagher spent some time during his own rehabilitation from polio, into his autobiography. Gallagher might be seen as having been on a continuum with

Roosevelt in that, in order to succeed in politics, Roosevelt was obliged to hide his disability and its challenges. To succeed at evaluating Roosevelt's physical challenges and facilitating changes for all people in the United States who have disabilities, Gallagher was obliged to make his struggles public. It is a component of life in the United States today: a shift away from the older, "Do as I say, not as I do," to greater accountability not only for people's words and actions in public, but the ways in which we truly live.

Shifting from Roosevelt and Gallagher, another example of a historical perspective in persuasive writing is one of my autobiographical essays, "The Roots from which I Move":

> Founded in 1870, St. Mary's is one of the premier hospitals in the world for children and adolescents with postacute illnesses and disabilities. I was a patient there from July 7, 1970, to June 25, 1971. There I received a general education in life that is available to few 10- and 11-year-olds. St. Mary's Healthcare System has diversified considerably since my time there. St. Mary's Hospital for Children is only one component of the system, which currently cares for young people to the age of 18 who are affected by disabling and postsurgical conditions, need post–organ transplant care, or have AIDS or other conditions of disability, illness, or trauma, including severe burns.

This first paragraph sets the scene with an explanation and some background information.

> Except for AIDS, which was not in the general population then, and organ transplant care, which likely would have been considered an acute medical condition in the early 1970s, the conditions that are treated are similar to those of 35 years ago, including the care of children with severe burns. My particular case was spastic cerebral palsy, and, after spending seven of my ten years in outpatient therapy departments and surgery in Rhode Island, my prescription in New York was intensive physical therapy. My therapist, with whom I worked two to three hours a day (and more after surgery in the autumn of 1970) was one of the most wonderful people I had encountered to date. The hallmark of the medical and therapy program at the hospital was as close to excellent as I had encountered, and it reflected not only the stellar caliber of the University Hospital, but the increased professionalism of rehabilitative medicine and therapy. Two examples of this were the training levels of social work and physical therapy:

to that time, both could be bachelor-level degrees. Those with master's degrees in social work and physical therapy were usually in administration, as were my Bayside therapist and a man who had been my physical therapist at a summer camp in Vermont the previous year. They supervised staffs but also were hands-on in therapy, to the great benefit of their patients. The further level of education, coupled with the younger generation's increasing awareness of and work for the civil rights of patients, made significant innovations possible. In Bayside, stretching and endurance-building exercises preceded sophisticated, difficult tasks such as walking with a walker or crutches.

The paragraph provides background information and a short lesson in the history of social work and physical therapy, but when do we get to the persuasion?

The woman who was Bayside's occupational therapist was Japanese. Each of our therapy sessions together began with hot tea with lemon and cookies. She, too, was a truly humane therapist. That had not necessarily been a given in the relative dark ages of my childhood. I found a sort of verbal justice at the age of nine in realizing that "therapist" could be split to be constructed "the rapist." I wasn't actually ever molested; however, in the sixties and, I assume, times prior to that decade, emotional and physical intimidation were common in the programs I had been in. Although the environment at St. Mary's was authoritarian and stratified, with a definite professional hierarchy that is common to hospitals—board of directors, consultant physician, upper-level physical and occupational staffs, lower level PT staff, nurses, and nurses' aides, all under the auspices of New York's University Hospital—emotional and physical maltreatment were relatively rare, especially among the upper-level staff.

For nearly a year, as my body was stretched, moved, and strengthened, my mind was as well, as for the first time in my life I encountered people from all strata of society and varying abilities and disabilities. For the first time I experienced the true healing power of laughter, when an eight-year-old girl who suffered from frequent, nearly critical asthma attacks relaxed to my jokes and stories after a day of staying in bed because of severe wheezing. For the first time I saw simultaneously one teenager recover from a paralyzing but temporary illness, as another, a beautiful redhead with green eyes, was close to death from a severely advanced case of multiple sclerosis. The embryonic conflict theorist in me perhaps had an inkling that I was experiencing a fairly large sample of human existence. St. Mary's was also the workplace of an order of Episcopal sisters, although nearly every ethnic and economic group, including some children from Europe who had been sent by their parents because of Bayside's reputation, was represented. Children of privilege ate, slept, and had occasional tantrums next to foundlings and children of abuse. The only noticeable difference in the treatment of the kids was in the length of time away that we that were allowed, since private insurance would pay for extended leaves—my most extended leave was about two weeks—and the state would accommodate only approximately 72 hours' leave before the child was considered to have been discharged from the hospital.

There it is—how and in what ways rehabilitation and treatment were focused in New York in the 1970s, and why it was significant. The reader is also getting to know something about the employees, children, and teens of St. Mary's Hospital, and this identification persuades the reader to care about the people.

Eighteen years elapsed, during which I visited St. Mary's only once, on a trip with my brother. At age 29 I was planning to begin a master's course in conflict management and decided to visit some friends in New York before leaving for the Center (now Institute) for Conflict Analysis and Resolution at George Mason University in Fairfax, Virginia. In addition, I would be able to stay in the Algonquin Hotel, the landmark of theater and popular literature that continues to be one of my favorite places in New York. As a child, I used to dream of being a writer and staying at the Algonquin; alas, I was born about 60 years too late to be among the Round Table group. The Round Table itself, though, was still on display.

When I visited in 1989, the headwaiter at the restaurant in the hotel seated the guests in the dining room pretty much according to the good their advertisement could do the establishment. He looked at me and decided I needed to be two or three tables away from any main lights. My entertainment during dinner was watching Matilda, the famous Algonquin cat, groom herself in the center of the dining room, near a Broadway producer and to the disgust of the headwaiter. The night before I had gone to the lobby to inquire about and try to see her, but she had been asleep on one of the mailbags.

The next night I had dinner in the dining room with two friends who were newlyweds of such social prominence that we were assigned a table that was one table away from a light. After an enjoyable dinner and making arrangements to meet them in a coffee house the next day, I went to my room. Deciding to see what the hotel's closed-circuit television channel offered, I was somewhat taken aback to see that holiday cards designed by the children at St. Mary's Hospital for Children were for sale in the lobby. At first I didn't know why I was so startled, then understood; the advertisement was a sharp reminder of the cyclical nature of life.

I had moved on and became an adult, but St. Mary's remained a part of my psyche.

This next section encompasses life as a young adult, after my experience at St. Mary's Hospital, as a public speaker as part of the tidal wave of information and discovery that occurred between the 1970s and the present. Parts of this story were included in a panel discussion in 1989 at Rhode Island College about job hunting successfully when disabled. The part that follows is from the original essay.

"How do you go to the bathroom?"
"How do you deal with barriers to employment?"
"How about relationships with men?"

What is going on here? Does this group of questions state a position or a fact? Yes, they do; in my teens and early 20s I made speeches, mostly for The Easter Seal Society of Rhode Island. My job in the 1970s and 1980s was to persuade people in the smallest state that people with disabilities led productive lives.

These and similar direct and indirect questions are some that I have been asked. I spoke on such topics principally between the ages of 12 and 25, after which my public speaking and writing turned increasingly to topics of research instead of daily life. Professional interviews, particularly those conducted with or by people whom I had just met, very often contain clues of personal questions that people want to ask, and I have become adept at reading them. In the United States, questions pertaining to geographic or ethnic origin, disability, religion, or nearly any other personal concerns are not allowed to be included in work-related interviews, other than in certain contexts for news interviews. There is nothing that precludes the person being interviewed from answering questions that are not asked; however, and I try to address this.

In persuasive speaking and writing, it helps to be able to anticipate what people may want to ask, but are emotionally or legally unable to ask.

"I expect that you are wondering about the wheelchair [in a given situation]. Well, here's what I do. . . ." I then proceed to explain how I function, maneuver, and so on, and I have found that the approach generally increases the potential or existing working harmony.

I was the first in my city to attend regular classes using a wheelchair in public school from first grade through high school. (As an aside, in the 1960s and at least half of the 1970s most bathrooms for students in those schools were not large enough to admit a wheelchair, so I trained myself not to need to go. It was good practice for transatlantic flights in later years.)

What was it like to go to school?

Circumstances necessitated my changing schools frequently: for increased intellectual stimulation, a year in New York, the end of elementary school, one year of junior high school, and then another change because the school students in my community attended was less accessible than another one in a different part of the city, and finally *three years* in high school—the most time that I had spent in one school. In all, eight changes in 12 years. The caliber of the teaching, particularly, varied considerably among the schools; I remember with great affection three excellent teachers—two of English and one of math—and with distaste one very poor English teacher cum guidance counselor and a math teacher who was biding her time until retirement.

My public speaking regarding life with cerebral palsy began as an inspiration of a friend of my sister, who was a teacher in junior high school in Jamestown, Rhode Island, circa 1971. He was arranging a series of lectures for his students of people who faced unusual situations in their lives. I had gone public before about cerebral palsy: I had been the Easter Seal Poster Child for Rhode Island in 1965 and spoke and interacted easily in groups. The junior high classes and I had an interesting day, during which I was asked a variety of questions about general function—getting around, and socializing. Four or five years later a more formal project was developed by two women in cooperation with the Easter Seal Society. This project had multiple phases during which the participants simulated conditions of various disabilities to gain a somewhat firsthand perspective on blindness, deafness, and learning and physical disabilities. The last phase of the project involved speakers, and I was invited to be one.

What is the point of this story? My early life was an object lesson in persuasion. I was one of the guinea pigs of my era to demonstrate that society could and should accept and help to facilitate people with disabilities going to school and to work.

That launched my part-time career as a public speaker. During the 1970s and early 1980s my speeches emphasized my functioning with a disability; after acquiring expertise and education in professions, however, I demurred from most talks about my personal life in favor of significant components of conflict theory and the varied research I conducted as a professional librarian.

One of the highlights of the 1980s was my passing the written Foreign Service examination. I had known this to be an achievement from my undergraduate days at Brown University: generally, one or two undergraduates passed the written exam every year, to continue to the oral exams at the Foreign Service Institute in Rosslyn, Virginia. When I passed, I was finishing a geography degree at Rhode Island College. A woman who was in a history master's degree program greeted me with praise and statistics: Did I know that only two percent of the people who took the written exam passed? I affirmed that I did; however, this had not been my first time to take it. Did I know that only two percent of the people who passed were women? I hadn't known that. It seemed a much smaller percentage than would be reasonable considering the number of female Foreign Service officers that there were at the time. At the micro level, although admittedly it was a tiny sample of an elite group, of the five people I had known of at Brown who had passed the written exam, two were women. Until the Americans with Disabilities Act of 1990 was passed, it was difficult to be hired by the Foreign Service if you were disabled.

I didn't pass all the stages of the examination process; however, I did have the opportunity to join the Foreign Service after Peace Corps work in the late 1990s. By then I opted to try life in Wales but was supremely gratified to see and be a part of the progress that had been made.

The Americans with Disabilities Act literally forced open the doors of private, city, state, and federal workplaces. Many human guinea pigs helped to make it happen.

The ADA's Impact

I had two jobs that required research and writing in succession while a student at the Simmons College Graduate School of Library and Information Science. One was as a research assistant for the Warburg professor of international relations, and the other was assistant to the associate dean of student life. In the latter capacity, I provided information on Simmons policies and practices as set down by Section 504 and the Americans With Disabilities Act of 1990 to the associate dean and students who requested it. Both laws address issues of education and employment for people with disabilities, and the ADA is the comprehensive law of the land regarding antidiscrimination. A year later, in the role of consultant to Simmons' Office of Student Life, I coordinated a conference focused on disability law and policies as they related to universities. At this conference, I also presented a paper with the catchy title, "Report on the ADA Guidelines."

My Role in Jamaica

A year after receiving my MSLIS degree, I went to Jamaica as a Peace Corps volunteer. My large project was to interview directors of agencies to find out what challenges they and their clients faced in providing and accessing resources. I also gave public health presentations in public places. Three of the more popular ones, which were later collected and distributed by the agency that I worked for, were "Disability is a Challenge . . . Or Is It?," which was presented first to the Clarendon Group for the Disabled in Clarendon, Jamaica in 1998; "Why Not Drugs?," presented to St. Hugh's Preparatory School in Kingston, Jamaica, in 1998; and "Seatbelt Safety," in Kingston, Jamaica, in 1999. The first presentation addressed basic issues of a person living and functioning in society when disabled. The second two described the realities of disability and death that can occur with drug abuse and the misuse or nonuse of car seatbelts.

While I was conducting my research on agencies, the Jamaica *Gleaner* published an article about the Jamaica Council for Persons with Disabilities, where I worked, and the research results to that time. The article, entitled "For Love of the Disabled," appeared in March 1998 and led to a meeting between Dr. Marigold Thorburn and myself. Dr. Thorburn was a powerhouse who had developed national programs and agencies from scratch. We felt that the development of a national coalition would answer the needs of the then-competing agencies. We began to develop forums to discuss this possibility with agency directors across the country.

The Jamaica Coalition on Disability was launched in June 1999 in Kingston by agency directors, medical personnel, representatives of the Jamaican Government and one of the United States Peace Corps volunteers (myself). Its two main goals were to end the competition for resources that had been necessary among the agencies and to increase their political leverage.

Separate surveys conducted by Dr. Thorburn and me some years prior to the development of the Coalition illustrated the challenges faced in providing goods and services to people with disabilities.

Dr. Thorburn's medical research and my nonmedical survey disclosed that chief among the challenges were the lack of resources for the agencies and the difficulty in access for the potential clients. Agencies gained resources via the government in competition with one another: for example, when the Society for the Blind was granted something, the Society for the Deaf was not.

Meetings were held between October 1998 and June 1999 to determine whether or not agency directors perceived a need for a national coalition of agencies to share resources and command the respect of the government by the numbers of people involved. (It is estimated that 15 percent of the people of Jamaica have one or more disabling condition or impairment.) At the final meeting representatives of 15 agencies voted for the coalition.

More than nine years have passed since the launch, and the coalition has been instrumental in introducing antidiscrimination legislation to Jamaica that is similar to the comprehensive Americans with Disabilities Act of 1990.

Following is a somewhat differently compiled version of a preface from a defunct Web page that Rebecca (Becky) Barton and I developed in 2006 to present a directory of physical and psychological access in Cardiff, Wales. Access for people with disabilities was incomplete in Wales. Although public policies encouraged education and employment, no law prohibited discrimination. Physical access existed in some places, but it varied in amount and quality from nonexistent to very good. Becky and I conducted the research to advertise the information to potential tourists and to increase people's sensitivity and awareness within Wales.

Becky and I received a range of input about the research that ran from dislike, to mild interest, to a request from a woman that I print out the text and send it to her. She had always felt embarrassed in public because people stared at her. She was particularly interested in the places that we defined as psychologically accessible.

In the following example, I explained to the readers first why the coauthor and I were qualified to write about this topic. In the second paragraph I explained briefly why the topic was significant. In the subsequent chapters, I explained how the topic had been structured for Web publication.

It comes as a surprise to us as the authors of this guide that we are supremely qualified for this task. We have had a combined 55 years' experience (Gulp! Becky Barton wants me to mention that I'm the older) pursuing physical access. Perceptions of access have made a difference in the quality of our lives—and sometimes a significant difference in its stress level. Some examples of this include my nearly being pushed down a flight of stairs that a well-meaning park ranger may have mistaken for a ramp in Washington, D.C.; and one that Becky Barton still laughs at—our looking at a possible flat for me to buy in Cardiff and the estate agent's pointing out the "convenient fire-escape"—a stairwell that led from the third to the ground floor.

The truth, of course, is that access is no joke. Physical access and its subtle partner, psychological access, make a statement about society. To evaluate it means in certain ways to measure the truth behind that statement: Is the society ready and able to include people who have disabilities in its day-to-day functions? The answers can be surprising. They frequently stem from the public's basic lack of exposure to people's normality outside of our disabilities and a lack of practice regarding what makes a structure physically and psychologically accessible. Of course, to increase access means to increase exposure. In this lies the education of society.

Access Cardiff—2007 is a directory and guide to accommodation, attractions, and amenities in Cardiff City Center and Cardiff Bay. Included as well are nearby places of particular interest to tourists. The level to which they are physically accessible and provide a warm, decent welcome to people who are disabled is assessed by the authors. The content is geared mostly to people with mobility impairments and those who use crutches, frames, mobility scooters, and wheelchairs. It is appropriate for people who are accompanied or unaccompanied. Where the authors are able to provide them, descriptions are given for people who have visual or aural impairments. We hope we have provided sufficient information to be of help to people who have these conditions. Links to sources that provide services are included, and in places where the access is incomplete, the level of what is available is indicated.

The first section is arranged in alphabetical subject order with an outline of places, using bullet points for quick reference. The second section is organized by area and includes fuller descriptions of the places and their environs. This guide will also be useful for people with other mobility considerations, such as vacationers who have children in strollers.

You may be saying to yourselves that in the last few examples you were loaded down with examples of people dealing with disabilities. Yes, that is so. In the first examples, Franklin Roosevelt and Hugh Gallagher were monumentally persuasive people, and their disabilities contributed significantly to their persuasiveness, because they were sensitized in personal ways to particular difficulties and challenges and used their own physical and emotional experiences to address the needs of others. In the last example, the autobiographical sketch describes my progression from one aspect of persuasion, public speaking, to persuasion and progress through the actions of going from high school to graduate school to employment. Interview techniques, group dynamics, the experience of the written Foreign Service examination, and work in the Peace Corps and Wales are also touched on. In the essay's description, the reader is shown these linkages briefly.

GRANT AND BUSINESS PROPOSALS

Grant-proposal writing is a combination of high art and comparable high stress. A number of sources map out how to structure proposals, and serious proposal writers, be it of books, grants, or any other type, should marginalize the social-science speak they learned in graduate school and look at formulas that get results. Funding organizations—for example, Michael and John Warburg's www.warbros.com—very often provide an outline for proposals on their Web sites. Organizations always provide guidelines and frequently offer help and information to grant writers. The Women's Archive of Wales, for example, received a significant cash award from a Heritage Lottery Fund (HLF) after many months of toil, sweat, and swearing, and one failed attempt, after someone from the HLF offered specific guidance for the archive's second attempt.

Writing for a Good Cause: The Complete Guide to Crafting Proposals and Other Persuasive Pieces for Nonprofits by Joseph Barbato and Danielle S. Furlich is a marvelous resource for proposal and grant writing. Among their many excellent points, the authors stress the importance of learning a foundation's guidelines and following them exactly.[28]

See the "Strategies for Success" chapter for more information and an example of a book prospectus. Whether submitted to literary agents or directly to publishers, book prospectuses and proposals are very important tools to convince their readers that a manuscript is worth considering. Structuring a truly persuasive proposal is vital. Similar to the grant proposal, book proposals have particular structures that literary agents and publishing houses describe in detail. As you look at my example and others, remember to look at the individual Web pages of the agents publishers, contact agents, and editors you plan to contact to clarify any ambiguous points and answer questions that are not addressed in any published format.

DEADLINE ANXIETY ("IF I HAD THREE MORE DAYS . . . ")

"Three more days" was a not-so-secret wish that was familiar to most of us in graduate school. I remember telling a favorite dean, "I have two articles for publication, a presentation, and a research paper all due this week!" I was asking for sympathy, not an extension. To the dean's credit, she said plainly, "Now you know what *we* face!" It was time for the writer in me to grow up.

For all of the pressure deadlines create, they can be merciful. Deadlines give writers and presenters structure and limits, which means that on a definite date the project must be finished. That knowledge contributes to the reality of the situation: if you have two weeks to prepare, you are limited in the amount of content you can write, so you must focus your research appropriately. On the other hand, if you are given a year or more, you can schedule the development of a truly detailed report.

Anxiety breeds fear, which in turn breeds the perception of inability. Following are a few methods for dealing with a looming deadline and writer's block. These methods are healthy methods to help writers to cope.

Exercise

Exercise is a tension reliever and stress reducer. Daily exercise ought to be incorporated regularly in a workday, with regular mini-breaks for standing up and stretching whenever possible. Exercise boosts blood circulation, which increases oxygen to all organs of the body, including the brain. Many Web pages and other resources offer suggestions for incorporating exercise into daily life. Vitamin-ex.com, for example, emphasizes specific benefits to the body and mind of walking and other aerobic exercise-

WebMD.com is another useful Web site that offers information on health topics ranging from workouts to nutrition; advice on making exercise a habit is particularly useful.[29]

DEVELOP A STRATEGY FOR COMPLETING YOUR WORK

When you know your topic, develop an outline, either a tight or a flexible one, depending on which suits you, for your report or essay. The chapter "Issues and Challenges" gives examples of outlines that enable writers and presenters to plug in facts, opinions, and transitional phrases to develop successful essays. One example analyzes my essay "Peace Conference in Turkey" for its persuasiveness. Basic structures for analytical and narrative essays can also apply to persuasive essays. As you develop your outline, develop a schedule for the time available for research and writing, any other work, recreation, and rest.

Focus on the work, not the clock. As you become involved with the work, relax a little about the time frame. Focus on the task and chip away at the work. Even a few sentences added consistently will help to develop your essay or article and perhaps stimulate you to think creatively about the project. For times when a writer is truly blocked and cannot sketch thoughts on paper, Kate Turabian suggests that "ideas simmer in the subconscious while they combine and recombine into something new and surprising."[30] Turabian suggests a change of activity for a short while to see if the writer can return to the project revitalized, able to "get back on track."[31]

If you have a choice of topics, choose one with which you are familiar and research it as thoroughly as you can, remembering your time frame. There is a story of the actor Sam Waterston, who was to play Abraham Lincoln in a PBS documentary. He was deeply moved to discover a letter of Lincoln's that revealed a depth of sensitivity of which Waterston had been unaware.[32] Research is educational and particularly enjoyable as you learn about your topic.

PERSUADING COLLEAGUES

Professional colleagues can be some of the most difficult people to write for. Relating experiences to peers can be liberating but a bit intimidating. The writer is addressing a readership that can critique from a position of knowing where the writer is coming from. The readers are eager for stimulating accounts that are entertaining, informative, and related to their experiences, needs, and aspirations. The problems can be finding an agent or publisher and collecting appropriate information. Following is an excerpt that may be useful to novice writers. It is from "The Mobile Librarian," from *Thinking Outside the Book: Essays for Innovative Librarians:*

> For those who have wondered about the lure of being a "foreign correspondent," I respond without hesitation that it can be edifying as well as fun. . . . On a previous trip (to Wales), I had been asked to write an article for the journal *Technicalities* about an international Graduate Summer School in Librarianship. When I returned I was asked by its then-editor Sheila Intner to continue with a series to be called, "Tales from Wales." Additionally, I continued with access issues about Jamaica and Wales. If you are new to the field or adding an area of expertise, a good beginning can be to contact the professors in your Graduate School of Library and Information Science for references to publications, or a direct submission if a particular professor is an editor or publisher of a journal.[33]

Frank and Lillian Gilbreth and Their "Therbligs"

Another type of colleague interaction that is unquestionably persuasive is the revealing riddle. In the early part of the 20th century, the business and marriage partners Frank and Lillian Gilbreth devised a strategy to deal with unjust claims from professional rivals.[34]

The originators of the field of motion study," the Gilbreths are celebrated for many engineering inventions and innovations developed to eliminate fatigue and increase work efficiency and productivity. "Therbligs" were 17 components in a motion cycle that they identified in any action: search, find, select, grasp, position, assemble, use, disassemble, inspect, transport loaded, pre-position for next operation, release load, transport empty, wait, wait (the Gilbreths defined the two "wait" components as "unavoidable delay"), rest, and finally plan.[35]

"Therblig" is "Gilbreth" spelled nearly backwards. Frank Gilbreth Sr. developed the term in an attempt to deal with scientific management's founder Frederick P. Taylor's disciples—engineers who worked for Taylor, promoted his methods, and sometimes disparaged those of the Gilbreths, or tried to take credit for the development of motion study. Frank Sr. imagined challenging a Taylor disciple in public by having the Taylor engineer write his therbligs backward on a blackboard. The reversal of the name was discovered before Gilbreth's envisioned scene could occur.

This method of naming a system to demonstrate originality does not answer every question of originality or authenticity, but it can be very effective when, as in the case of the Taylorites, the rivals themselves used the term as their own without realizing its hidden meaning.

Research reveals a wide range of information that may be updated frequently or newly discovered. Investigation into a topic may result in an unexpected wave of information that can be transmitted to an audience that may, in turn, augment the work with experiences of its own. The result is an interactive dynamic experience. Barry Lane makes an important point about maintaining genuine and unique qualities in writing: "All energy in a piece of writing is equal to the play quotient of the writer squared. If a writer has no sense of play, the prose will be lifeless and anemic, as though anyone could have written it."[36]

Lane also recommends ways to encourage students' creativity in collecting information, and suggests an informal, alternative approach called "We-Search," which is described in a later section. Lane recommends focusing on strengths to deal with large, intimidating situations. He gives an example of his sketching Pharaoh Tutankhamen's funeral mask and other artifacts in a notebook to help him experience and remember an overwhelming amount of Egyptian art. The rediscovered sketches, found years later, brought back the memory of the gold room of relics more effectively for him than if he had tried to memorize everything during his visit.[37]

Lane recommends keeping a notebook to write down lists of story ideas and sketches to bring back vivid memories. He also recommends keeping what Dave Barry calls "Wisdom Lists,"[38]—little nuggets of truth that can be put into a sentence each. One of mine is, "The uselessness of a person's offer of help is proportional to the amount of time that she spends whining about herself." Other categories of items Lane suggests recording in a notebook include clippings, photos, and other artifacts, such as a speeding ticket that led to a funny exchange with a Vermont state trooper; imponderable questions, such as "Where do we go when we die?" or "What is peace?"; life gems and quotes; silly what-ifs; and spectacular to-do lists.[39] The motivation for keeping a notebook is not only to enhance memories but also to stimulate all types of thoughts and creativity. Ultimately, the solution is to not be afraid to seek eccentric sources or shy away from funny, interesting experiences. Savor them, and allow your audiences and readers to also.

Following is a creative exercise I wrote in 2006 to stimulate other parts of my memory as a break from conducting research. It helped to motivate me to continue my "real" work. I recommend this system to any writers when they are bored or blocked by one subject. You may find release by switching topics briefly: putting aside the frustrating work and writing about something that was fun.

PLAYERS' LESSONS

Before the age of 14, I was aces at giving birth. My debut in labor was at an audition for the Providence Players' reading of *Telemachus Clay*. My breathing, straining, and groaning won me a part in the production (although not that particular role!), and I was baptized into the Players. The amateur theater group mounted a production approximately every six weeks, and a Young People's Workshop for teenagers gave a performance in the spring under the direction of the multifaceted professional actress extraordinaire, Marilyn Meardon. This gifted actress and teacher was recognized in 2004 for her many contributions to performance art in Rhode Island by being awarded the Tom Robert's Prize for Creative Achievement in the Humanities.

Marilyn's strength was and is improvisation, and she taught us multiple ways and means of improvisation. She dwelt then as now in the realm of the imagination—it has become something of a byword phrase for her—and influenced a number of her students to go into acting successfully. As a mother and improviser, Marilyn was adept at dealing with teenagers. I am surprised at how well we behaved, but most of us were steeped in theater and cinema history and would tell each other chilling tales of Louis B. Mayer diets and the indentured servitude we imagined was typical of the lives of Broadway thespians—well, we *were* theatrical kids, of course. Compared to that, Marilyn's direction was gentle and inclusive. She even looked for value in most of our flubs: one of note involved a murder mystery that was performed by a small group of the students for the larger group. It was set on a train that was a far song from the *Orient Express*—a row or two of fold-up chairs. When the dimmed lights were turned on to reveal the freshly murdered body, one of the girls on stage let out such a hysterical squeal that we all burst out laughing. Marilyn used the incident to illustrate a lesson: you see, she pointed out, they developed the tension well and the scream was a release, coupled by the fact that you don't know how you'll react if you suddenly see a dead body.

It all made sense.

In addition to performing for one another, we engaged in small-group exercises. Everyone, even the tech people—those who were in charge of lighting, the stagehands, and others, who were not keen about acting—was obliged to do some group and stage work. A standard exercise was "mirror," during which in pairs you concentrated on each other's faces while first one, then the other, mimicked the other's motions. Another, again in pairs, was an improvised scene in which we were given a framework and created lines to tell the story.

Marilyn had a guest actor or director from a professional company in Rhode Island give a lesson at least once a season. Once, most of the group was to sit in a long line with arms linked and stand up simultaneously. It was decided that we needed a phrase other than the standards "help," or "ouch," in case people were in real pain or trouble and needed the group to stop. The phrase selected was "orange juice," and it prevented a girl's spraining her arm when the line began to move too quickly for her.

The piece des resistance was a group of plays that we performed for the public at the end of the workshops. Two of these were *The Crystal Apple* and a Baba Yaga folktale from Russia entitled *Vasalisa,* which of course became *Vasaline* to us immediately. In the latter I played the grandmother, Babushka, and can remember most of my lines now—something I wasn't always able to do when it was important—but, when in doubt, improvise, was an unofficial motto of our group. I remember one scene in another play in which Claire Beckman, who is now a veteran of theater and television, as a wily rabbit, and I, as a would-be wily wolf or fox, had to meet each other's eyes at the end of a group of lines. The main challenge in those giggly years was for us to keep our faces straight. Usually we could, to the relief of our director.

In addition to my theatrical endeavors in Providence, I also performed monologues on Saturday nights at eight o'clock for my family and whoever was, er, lucky enough to be visiting. Then in junior high school, I would look at a few books of one-act plays from the library and adapt dialogues from Sir James M. Barrie, Noel Coward, and others to suit my performances, or make up original work, sometimes with a "guest artist" from Marilyn's workshop. Of those I adapted I especially liked the larger works—at 14, my personal favorite was the Victorian interpretation of *The Barretts of Wimpole Street.* I didn't charge admission to these performances and so don't believe I was actually messing about with the copyrights, but being creative.

Research to Provide Information and Assistance

Sensitive issues that are common to a profession to which the colleague/ author has some options for possible solutions are stimulating, but sometimes intimidating, to address. The authors' and presenters' backgrounds should, as with any other issue of authority, demonstrate expertise in the area and an ability to address the situation effectively and with an understanding of the problems that their colleagues are facing. Following is the outline of a presentation that was sponsored by the Office of Library and Information Services of Rhode Island.

> This presentation has evolved through at least four incarnations. At first I envisioned it as a sort of presentation to the public of my experiences as a librarian/researcher who has worked in a variety of venues and uses a wheelchair—what issues and challenges I have encountered as a patron who uses libraries and online resources in her work, and as a librarian who has been responsible for access issues and facilitated coalition building. The next concept that occurred to me was that some time spent discussing the challenges and problems we have faced as librarians with limited budgets who must try to please all of the people all of the time would be good: a time of debriefing in a nonthreatening environment. The focus, though, needed refining: Louise Moulton of the Providence Public Library suggested that my presentation evolve as a conversation among librarians, and that the Office of Library and Information Services would be the appropriate sponsor. I am grateful to Louise, Howard Boksenbaum, Donna Longo DiMichele, and particularly Karen Mellor for enabling this forum to be. The fourth incarnation of this workshop's concept came to me in a rising tide through years of talking to librarians, and particularly in this past year: what we all need to know about, beyond our responsibilities to Section 504 of the Rehabilitation Act of 1973 and the Americans with Disabilities Act, is how to find and obtain funding effectively, so that quest constituted the majority of my research.

INTRODUCTION

This presentation will explain the relevant portions of the Americans with Disabilities Act and Section 504 as they relate to libraries and the reasons librarians and library staff should be familiar with the specifics and how to maintain them.

SCOPE AND PURPOSE

I plan to present examples of obstacles and challenges to patrons with disabilities, including computer access and use, and ways to deal with them. Additionally, I will present a brief analysis of the history of and reasons for acts and how they apply to research settings and libraries.

AUDIENCE
Rhode Island librarians and other library employees

MATERIALS
The relevant sections and examples of the ADA and Section 504, and examples of libraries' implementing and sustaining them will be projected and distributed to the audience.

CONCLUSION
Discussions with the audience about the sections, then question, answer and example time to follow.[40]

The presentation evolved from my introduction into a discussion about specific Americans with Disabilities Act requirements and recommendations for libraries. Many of the participants were interested and in need of information about funding sources. They took handouts of information with them, but their greater need was for me to clarify some areas of confusion and get information about the law itself. Because my focus was on funding, I had not prepared to discuss all of the aspects of the law, although I had handouts available of the categories in libraries that the ADA addresses and synopses of what the law recommends for each category. Additionally, I had handouts of funding and information resources compiled by the New Jersey State Library. Presentations can develop in unexpected ways, and it is beneficial to let the audience tell the presenter what its members need to know. Our solution in this case was to develop an online forum for librarians through the Office of Library and Information Services in Rhode Island, where I could read questions and post additional information. Online forums are particularly effective as sources of information that are readily available and interactive. The presenters have swift access to questions, clarifications, follow-up comments, and feedback, so can adjust their information and follow-up comments appropriately.

The initial presentation finished with my urging the audience to interpret the Americans with Disabilities Act as a vehicle of inclusion that benefits all America and that its mandate is that what can be done needs to be done.

In an appendix to *Why We Must Run with Scissors*, Diane Cyr quotes lawyer Alan Dershowitz saying, "Advocacy is not overpowering your opponent, . . . It's persuading your opponent that your ideas are his."[41] In a statement that reinforces the points about researching an audience and getting to know about them, Dershowitz says of opponents in legal cases,

"Don't believe you're going to make yourself seem smarter than they are, or better than they are, . . . Assume they're smarter than you are, they're righter than you are, they believe in their position as much as you do or more, they're as nice as you are."[42]

You will be more effective as an author, presenter, attorney, professor, physician, and in nearly any other role if you take the part as a participant instead of a boss. Remember that you will learn much about how effective your work has been by receiving and reviewing input from your audience.

"WE-SEARCH" VERSUS RESEARCH

Barry Lane, a teacher-development guru who is the author of many books on the art and craft of teaching writing to young students, advocates the incorporation of "we-search"—interaction with others, puns, jokes, hidden meanings, and other really enjoyable exercises (for example, he posts lines from a textbook, has students read them and then look away, think about the meanings of the sentences, and phrase their thoughts in their own words)[43]—to teach children and teenagers to think and write more effectively. The acid test was, did we-search really work as a teaching method?

Yes, was the resounding answer!

Barry Lane reports,

> Dr. Darla Shaw, a professor at Western Connecticut State University, found that just one wacky we-search paper assignment addressed between 25 and 30 of the state's performance standards. Not only that, the graduate students found the assignments to be enjoyable. In their closing essays, they said that doing wacky we-search was the most engaging assignment they had done in six years of college. Though students might not do wacky we-search papers in life, the thinking and writing skills that they learn as a result prepare them for success in the 21st century.[44]

That's persuasive evidence!

LOGICAL FALLACIES

In the study of logic, there are many types of logical fallacies or errors of logic. In persuasive writing, the avoidance of fallacies means to check your facts to avoid the type of structure below:

All spiders have eight legs.
Most quartets have eight legs.
Most quartets are spiders.

A persuasive argument is effective when it follows some form of logic, although, as Barry Lane and Gretchen Bernabei have demonstrated in their works cited in this chapter, it can be eccentric logic with premises that oppose what is expected. Check the structure of your argument not only for clarity, but common sense.

Following are some excerpts from an episode at Brown University in Providence, Rhode Island, in 1982. The planning of the weekend was full of potential pitfalls and problems that turned into solutions in unexpected ways. The event involved a lot of persuasion, and I report it as I recall it.

I don't take any but the mildest credit for what happened that weekend. As a facilitator, all I did was issue the invitations and make some announcements and pertinent puns. The real miracle took place behind the scenes between the true key players who made it possible.

Anyone who studied international relations in the years between Hitler's death and Gorbachev's election knew the omnipresence of the adverse relationship between the U.S.S.R. and U.S.A. China nudged in there to give each a fickle ally from time to time; however, for the better part of 40 years, there was a feeling that the Cold War was, if not here to stay, at least to chill for awhile.

There were explanations and interpretations galore, and among the better analysts was a Kremlinologist and former United States ambassador to Poland, Richard T. Davies. He was a man of a multitude of parts. The language genius and well-trained analyst was someone who cared passionately about many things, from the environment, to the survival and functions of nations and peoples, to personal reputations, to his prowess at tennis.

He reached a particular level of achievement in his career in government when in 1972 President Richard M. Nixon named him ambassador to Poland. Dick retired from the Foreign Service in 1980. He and his wife, Jean, claimed that they had been "to every country but China."

Dick's expertise was called upon by many in the early 1980s to interpret the goings-on in Gdansk, particularly the organization and development of the Solidarity Labor Union. One of the people to entice him out of his nest to come north and speak to some young folks in Providence—and, it would turn out, to some older folks as well—was an international-relations student at Brown University who realized that if Dick could speak in mid-April 1982 the date would coincide nicely with his youngest son's 21st birthday. Dick's youngest son was also a Brown student. I had contacted Dick for the first time in February 1981 to ask him if he felt that it was likely that the Soviet Union would invade Poland, and he responded that the U.S.S.R. would not be likely to invade since it couldn't afford Poland's debt.

I needed the approval of the proposed speaker, then of the president of the John Hay Society, which was a group of students who had international relations and political science concentrations. Davies was amenable and agreed immediately. The head honcho of John Hay, not realizing there was a particular significance to the April date, wanted him at another time and was bewildered when I told him we had to keep that date. He moaned loudly that John Hay had booked Thomas Watson, Harold Brown, and Richard Davies close together, with diminishing treasury funds. What were we to do? A few times in a life span there are moments such as these. I replied, "We can advertise them together as not just any Tom, Dick, and Harry." I was rewarded, after a second's pause, by a burst of long laughter, and the president relaxed after this. He told me we could pay Dick only about a tenth of his usual fee and no expenses. I said I thought that would be all right (and it was). As a friend of mine pointed out later, of course I was able to persuade Dick to come; I had a hostage. Well, I didn't, but perhaps Brown did.

Just as Davies reconciled himself to a stipend, a long drive, and crashing for the night in a friend's apartment, Brown's Center for Foreign Policy contacted him and asked, well, if he were coming to speak to the kids, might he speak to the center the night before? *They would pay him what the John Hay Society paid.* Whether Dick's inherent honesty came to the fore, or the Center knew what we were paying him I never knew; however, for years I had an uncomfortable, self-inflicted feeling that I owed him some money.

It all went well that Thursday to Saturday, except for about ten minutes on Friday afternoon when I couldn't see Dick at our meeting place and it turned out that he was intentionally hiding behind me. That weekend is a time I would like to relive, although the second time around with more cash for the gracious man who gave a serious speech twice, and in doing so demonstrated his love for his son and charity and tolerance for the rest of us.

For additional examples of solutions to apply to persuasion, see chapter 4, "Strategies for Success."

NOTES

James Cash Penney, *QuotationsBook*, quotationsbook.com/quote/32502/ Staff, eds. (it is logical that someone with the names Cash Penney would be good in business, and the founder of the J. C. Penney department store chain fulfilled the promise, although his cash worth totaled considerably more than pennies); Anthony Robbins, Anthony Robbins' Famous Quote About Energy, Power, Solutions, Inspiration/Quotes Dadd, www.quotes daddy.com/quote/1387489/Anthony+Robbins/identify-your-problems-but-give-your-power-and-energy; John Steinbeck, *Creative Quotations from John Steinbeck: (1902–1968) born on Feb. 27*, creativequotations.com/one/1817b.htm.

1. Kate L. Turabian, *A Manual for Writers of Research Papers, Theses, and Dissertations*, 7th ed. (Chicago: The University of Chicago Press, 2007), 77.

2. Ibid., 80.

3. Ibid., 80.

4. *The Essential Writer's Companion: A Concise Guide to Writing Effectively for School, Home or Office* (New York: Houghton Mifflin, 1997), 221.

5. Carolyn Davis, "Survey on Agencies," presentation to the Committee of Disability Service Agencies, Kingston, Jamaica, June 2, 1998.

6. Vincent Wilson Jr. and Gale S. McClung, *The Book of Distinguished American Women* (Brookeville, MD: American History Research Associates, 2003), 64.

7. Ibid., 64.

8. Sunshine for Women Web site, "Sarah Grimke (1792–1873) and Angelina Grimke Weld (1805–1879) Letters on the Equality of the Sexes 1838 Letters to Catherine e. Beecher 1837," www.pinn.net/~sunshine/whm2000/grimke4.html.

9. Wilson and McClung, *The Book of Distinguished American Women*, 64.

10. Sunshine for Women.

11. Ibid.

12. Ibid.

13. Wilson and McClung, *The Book of Distinguished American Women*, 64.

14. Barry Lane and Gretchen Bernabei, *Why We Must Run With Scissors: Voice Lessons in Persuasive Writing 3-12* (Shoreham, VT: Discover Writing Press, 2001), 174.

15. Brainyquote. "James Thurber Quotes," www.brainyquote.com/quotes/quotes/j/jamesthurb107156.html.

16. Lane and Bernabei, *Why We Must Run With Scissors*, 60.

17. Carolyn Davis, e-mail message, June 14, 2009.

18. The History Place Great Speeches Collection, "Tony Blair Address to the Irish Parliament." www.historyplace.com/speeches/blair.htm.

19. Ibid.

20. Ibid.

21. Ibid.

22. "Obama's Victory Speech," news.bbc.co.uk/1/hi/world/americas/us_elections_2008/7710038.stm.

23. Ibid.

24. Ibid.

25. "Timothy Hughes, Rare and Early Newspapers" Catalog 162, and Walt Kelly, creator of *Pogo*, www.pogopossum.com.

26. Elie Wiesel, *Night* (New York: Hill and Wang, 2006), 5.

27. Hugh Gregory Gallagher, *Disabled in an Able-Bodied World* (Arlington, VA: Vandamere Press, 1998), 78–79.

28. Joseph Barbato and Danielle S. Furlich, *Writing for a Good Cause: The Complete Guide to Crafting Proposals and Other Persuasive Pieces for Nonprofits* (New York: Simon & Schuster, 2000), 88.

29. Leanna Skarnulis, "Women's Health: 10 Easy Ways to Make Exercise a Habit—Try These Tricks to Become One of the Fitness Faithful," www.webmd.com/fitness-exercise/guide/exercise-habits.

30. Turabian, *A Manual for Writers*, 81.

31. Ibid., 81.

32. *Memory and Imagination: New Paths to the Library of Congress*, video.google.com/videosearch?hl=en&q=memory+and+imagination:+new+pathways+to+the+library+of+congress&um=1&ie=UTF-8&sa=X&oi=video_result_group&resnum=4&cttitle#.

33. Carolyn Davis, "The Mobile Librarian," in *Thinking Outside the Book: Essays for Innovative Librarians*, ed. Carol Smallwood (Jefferson, NC: McFarland Publishers, 2008), 235–236.

34. Frank B. Gilbreth Jr., *Time Out for Happiness* (New York: Thomas Y. Crowell Company, 1970), 153.

35. Ibid., 153.

36. Barry Lane, *But How Do You Teach Writing?: A Simple Guide for All Teachers* (New York: Scholastic Teaching Resources, 2008), 61.

37. Ibid., 62.

38. Ibid., 63–64.

39. Ibid., 64–66.

40. Carolyn Davis, "ADA Section 504 Outline for the Office of Library and Information Services," presentation given at the Warwick Public Library, Warwick, Rhode Island, April 28, 2009.

41. Diane Cyr, "How to Argue: Interview with Alan Dershowitz," in *Why We Must Run With Scissors*, ed. Lane and Bernabei, 255.

42. Ibid.

43. Lane, *But How Do You Teach Writing*, 31, 127; Barry Lane, *51 Wacky We-Search Reports: Face the Facts with Fun* (New York: Discover Writing Press).

44. Lane, *But How Do You Teach Writing?*, 31.

CHAPTER 4

Strategies for Success: Everything That Attracted Me to Reading Reports for School, College, and Business I Learned by the Fourth Grade

How far you go in life depends on your being tender with the young, compassionate with the aged, sympathetic with the striving and tolerant of the weak and strong. Because someday in your life you will have been all of these.

—George Washington Carver

I LIKED THIS REPORT BECAUSE IT WAS INTERESTING

What is your writing talent? Is it the clear presentation of information? The easy flow of one sentence to another? The ability to offer unique perspectives? Humor? Brevity? All of the above? Whatever your writing talents are, you will have more deeply engaged readers if you use them well. How do you develop your writing talents? By learning and practicing good grammar and sentence structure; by writing frequently, preferably daily; and by reading good material. Well-presented material entertains and informs you, and reading a variety of it will help you to develop and sharpen your craft.

Interesting writing tells a story well. As noted, persuasive writing incorporates facts—which can be places, personal experiences, observations, and researched information—and emotion to convince readers of a point of view. When reporting a situation that you have been involved in, what do your senses of touch, taste, smell, hearing, and sight take in? How do you process the information and what is your reaction to it? How can your readers understand the experience? What do you expect them to think and feel about it? Will some commentary add to or detract from the persuasiveness of your writing?

Does the following passage get your attention?

> First, from inside, came the stench of urine. It hit us as we got out of the Peace Corps car and walked/rolled towards Strathmore House, an unregistered children's home in Jamaica where one of us would work for the next two years. Strathmore House was somewhat under the auspices of the Peace Corps in Jamaica, which meant that we sent volunteers there and tried to help out in cleaning and maintaining the place, but it was never nearly enough. The lack of adequate personnel, and a dearth of training for and motivation of those who worked there, meant that neglect and filth, and the accompanying worms and other parasites, were a way of life for the disabled people who stayed there. There were about 40 in a house that could have held about 8, and they ranged in age from babies of a couple of months to young adults of about 20 years. Strathmore's owner had intended it to be an orphanage and a haven; for disabled people it had turned into a hellhole. The able-bodied children and young people fared better as they were better able to care for themselves; however, everyone was vulnerable to parasites and general neglect.[1]

In this introductory paragraph, I am illustrating and describing my observations and experiences in a particular setting at a particular time to explain my point of view and to direct, even shock, the reader into the same mindset. Notice the use of the words *stench, urine, neglect, filth, worms, parasites* and *hellhole*. These are shockers intended to leave no room for ambiguity and to prepare the way for the additional descriptions that follow.

The following paragraph reports briefly why Strathmore House had so few resources and how the volunteer affected the structure of the house. It is written from the first-person plural perspectives to describe and engage the readers in others' points of view and actions.

> When asked about applying for additional funding to enable the hiring of trained personnel, the owner tended to respond that "The Lord would

provide." While we tried to respect her convictions, we felt that her attitude was perhaps engendered by exhaustion. Bit by bit, with the backing
of Peace Corps and whatever moral and physical support we, the other
volunteers could give, the volunteer who was assigned there tried to introduce changes in hygiene, give attention and affection to the youngsters,
and introduce and encourage—gently and more patiently than many of
us could have—changes in attitudes and habits toward those with disabilities.[2]

In this excerpt, more stories about the residents add detail and give more
life to the story.

I can remember many times when the children, who were starved for affection and comfort, jumped into any woman's arms to be cuddled and
soon came to know that visits from what must have seemed to them
strangely colored and shaped people meant attention and sweet treats,
as well as a lot of cleaning.

My most enduring memory is of a young woman who was lying on the
floor of the terrace of the house—her eyes, intellect, and speech clear,
talking to me about her illness. Her body, in sharp contrast to her mind,
was completely wasted and emaciated, and she couldn't move by herself. Whether that condition was caused or exacerbated by the conditions at Strathmore I don't know, but we were able to do little to ease her
suffering. Many people in the world are abandoned and neglected, but
when a person who has been treated in that way speaks to you about it
in calm, rational tones, it has an impact that is difficult to define   and
impossible to forget.[3]

The tone shifts back to the first-person singular and the impact the experience had on me, the writer. The previous paragraph's structure yields
to the structure and tone that were used at the beginning of the vignette.

The summary begins in the next paragraph by stating briefly the status
of Strathmore House to the Peace Corps and an admonition to readers.

Strathmore is no longer under the auspices of the Peace Corps. This story
doesn't have a conclusion, and I don't pretend that Strathmore House encompasses the worst of existences for people even in Jamaica, let alone
the world. However, it is an experience that few Americans or people of
the European Union will ever have, because laws, policies, and funding

prohibit that degree of neglect. We need to be aware that not only does it exist but that it also exists truly in the guise of caring for others.[4]

In the final paragraph I wrap up this specific story with a warning to the audience to be wary of underfunded would-be philanthropy, and expand the situation to the Jamaican national level.

> The care of orphans and children who are abandoned, especially those whose situations include disabling conditions, can be uneven. Although registered children's homes must by Jamaican law comply with some established standards, there are many unregistered orphanages that function poorly because the founder/director is unable to provide service, facilities, caregivers, space, or time, because of the scarcity of resources. The results are often unacceptable for the growth and development of children and young adults. The number of informal orphanages in Jamaica and the number of children in them is difficult to document. They answer to no agency and no particular funding bodies. The lack of action, initiative, or sometimes concern by those in authority, who are, admittedly, overworked and understaffed, allows the neglect to continue. Directors of registered agencies echoed similar problems: trained personnel attract funding; however, an agency requires funding to attract the trained personnel in the first place. Children frequently do not have access to medical care; as a result, diseases of the thyroid and nervous system and various viruses stay unchecked, causing the increasing impairment and wasting of young bodies.[5]

I LIKED THIS REPORT BECAUSE THE WRITER KNEW THE AUDIENCE

A local author spoke recently to an audience comprised mostly of publishers, editors, and librarians, some of whom were authors also. After a lengthy introduction describing how her first book was published, she rounded off that part of her talk by informing us that perhaps even *we* might be able to write. It was obvious beyond the patronizing tone that she wasn't aware of her audience, and much of her talk, therefore, was inappropriate. Librarians' relationship to writing is similar to physicians' knowledge of childbirth. Even those who have not actually participated firsthand know a good amount about the process.

To help earn and keep your audience's respect for your informed presentation or article, conduct some research before you submit your proposal for an article or book or write your presentation. What ages and genders (including self-identified genders) of people are going to read your work? What types and levels of knowledge are they likely to have of your subject(s)? What is the journal, publishing house, university, school, or organization planning for your work? If it is to be published, which markets or niches are to be targeted? The success of an essay, chapter, or book has much to do with its being geared to the appropriate market. Editors and publishers will help you with information, guidelines, and suggestions; however, it is crucial that you do your own homework. Researching the audience is more important if you are writing an essay or report for school, university, or graduate work, or for a business presentation, than an article or book for publication, as you will probably receive less advance information in the latter situation—unless you are submitting your work to only one person, but even then, it helps to know something about that person's expectations.

Having received the guidelines from your teacher, editor, team leader, or supervisor, you should next conduct some additional research on your own. If you are developing a presentation to be delivered orally, you can state some of your assumptions to your audience, and see how they respond, for example, "I assume that you've all read Harper Lee's *To Kill a Mockingbird*," or, "I assume that you all know the main provisions of Public Law 94–142." It is important to state your assumptions in ways that won't alienate your audience or readers, so general statements are frequently safer than specific ones; however, there may be times when specific questions or statements are desirable. Some examples are, "If you look at the bibliographic references cited in this work you will note that the late Kenneth Boulding's work is referred to frequently. It is essential to have a good grounding in Professor Boulding's work to evaluate my research and conclusions." And, from a guest speaker, "I assume that everyone here is training for teacher certification and that you all have had more academic experience as students than as teachers." You can state assumptions in written presentations as well, of course. In most cases you will not receive the feedback as quickly or as spontaneously, but your written assumptions can serve as guides to the validity of your assumptions, and your audience will know something about the perspective from which you wrote your essay or report.

The veteran writers and persuaders Linda Bridges and William F. Rickenbacker wrote of the essayist José Ortega y Gasset, the author of more than 20 books, that for all of the delineation of style in his work, ultimately Ortega's success as an author rested in his primary emphasis on the reader.[6] Ortega wrote that, "Style is the deformation of the common tongue for the special purposes of the speaker."[7] This entrancing thought can be applied to the writer as well. Invest yourself in appropriate communication with your audience and you will be more successful than if your primary focus is on yourself. The writer–reader relationship should consist of similar components of interest, courtesy, and connection that are common to any functional relationship.

A large component of knowing readers or an audience is knowing how to communicate with them. An example of appropriate communication is a mathematics teacher instructing a classroom of students whose strengths are verbal. It is important for the teacher to emphasize verbal instruction throughout the lesson, despite the temptation to use mathematical shorthand. For example, the equation "$f(x)-y = 36$" is better translated to "The function of x minus y, when y equals (or "is set to") 0, is 36" for such an audience.

I LIKED THIS REPORT BECAUSE THE AUTHOR KNEW THE SUBJECT

At every level, from school to the professions, there are competent and incompetent writers and editors. If you are to be taken seriously and to be considered competent, you must be familiar with your subject area. You demonstrate this by consulting other professionals and colleagues, researching your topic appropriately, and using appropriate terms in the context of your writing.

Persuasive writing is essential in many formats, including query letters and grant and book proposals. These vehicles follow fairly rigid structures and demand that certain precise information be included.

Grant Writing and Business Proposals In *Writing for a Good Cause: The Complete Guide to Crafting Proposals and Other Persuasive Pieces for Nonprofits*, authors Barbato and Furlich stress the importance of following a foundation's guidelines exactly. Their mandates include this basic but vital issue:

> You must check the [foundation that you are writing the grant for] guidelines before you start. . . .
> Why?
>
> • Because a 1990 survey by the *National Society of Fund Raising Executives Journal* found that the top complaint by foundation program officers is that grant seekers don't follow foundation guidelines.

- Because [Barbato and Furlich's] survey of the top 100 foundations in America revealed the exact same complaint.
- Because you will certainly be turned down if you do not follow the grantmaker's guidelines.
- Because you will at best annoy, and at worst forever alienate, the grantmaker if you can't follow even the simplest directions—that is, the guidelines.[8]

So, to summarize: *follow the guidelines!* And, as Barbato and Furlich also emphasize, when you need guidance, ask the grantmakers (I like to use the term "grant granters") for information.[9]

THE QUERY LETTER OR PROSPECTUS

Another form of proposal writing is one that is specific to authors: the book or article proposal. But before submitting a book proposal, a prospective author's first contact with a literary agent or publisher may be a query letter or e-mail. The message contains the author's background information, emphasizing expertise in the field or authority for the project, and a general description and outline of the manuscript: the topic, sources used, proposed table of contents, and proposed length. Following is a sample:

I am expanding my unpublished manuscript entitled *Power Relationships between the English and Welsh in the Principality of Wales: 1284–1415*. It is a cross-disciplinary text of medieval Welsh history and group/systems conflict theory that was researched and written in Cardiff, Wales.

Aspects of intra- as well as intergroup conflict in power relationships are examined between the English and Welsh of the Principality of Wales circa 1284–1415. Many theories and observations of social and Welsh historians are cited. The works of conflict theorists and criminologists Kenneth Boulding, George Vold, and Richard Quinney and others are applied and expanded. In particular, Boulding's and Vold's theories from the early modern and contemporary periods, respectively, are applied to late 13th- to early 15th-century Wales, particularly to the lands that came under royal control after the Principality's annexation to the English Crown in the early 1280s. After the introduction in Chapter I, the categories under discussion are society and economy in Chapter II; law, politics, and administration in Chapter III; and prophecy and religion in Chapter IV.

The table displays the table of contents and a list of my publications and presentations. The estimated word count will be 75,000.

Thank you for your consideration.

CONTENTS

Once you have received a positive response to your query letter, the next step is to provide the publisher or agent with a developed book proposal or prospectus that describes the proposed manuscript in detail. In addition to the information in the query letter, you should include a tentative title; a rationale, which is the subject and reason for writing the manuscript; the scope and purpose, which explains why people will be interested in it and how the work will be structured; the proposed audience, that is, every group that will buy it—specific age groups, professions, and so on. Competing works are very important to include in the form of an annotated bibliography, including prices!

Here is a sample of a proposal for a guide. The names and titles have been changed.

PROSPECTUS FOR AN INDEXING GUIDE SUBMITTED TO FREDERICK SMYTHE OF REDWOOD PUBLISHING

Tentative Title

Indexing: How to Succeed in Work and at School

Rationale

This book is intended to be part of the Redwood Indexing Guides. This guide will describe and demonstrate all forms of proper indexing. Examples from journals, series, books, and international library formats will be described and illustrated.

Scope and Purpose

The proposed work will be focused on a large segment of the population. The chapters will be divided into subheadings and discuss how and when to index. Examples of obstacles and challenges in a variety of formats of written presentations and ways to deal with them will be discussed. A history of indexing in the United States and the European Union will be included.

Audience
The guide is intended for authors, editors, indexers, librarians, and publishers.

Competing Works
Indexing Can Be Fun: A Practical Guide to Indexing Books and Journals. Spencer Wallis, IND Publishing, 2009, 360 pp., 24.95. An indexing guide for authors. My proposed work will not focus solely on books.

A History of European Indexing. James Smith, Print and Find Publications, 2000, 100 pp., $19.95. This book is brief and describes a basic history of indexing in Western Europe from 1900 to 1990. My proposed work will be a guide for many methods of indexing and will focus on a larger audience.

A Guide to Indexing for Books, Journals, or Libraries. Editors of Indexing Dictionaries, Indexing Muffin, 1991, 270 pp., (no price available). A comprehensive instruction manual for students, families and professionals that includes segments on indexes.

Is 1950 Included?: The Art and Science of Comprehensive Indexing. B&D Mauve, 2001, 220 pp., $13.95. This book is well constructed for many types of indexing.

Selling Points
The selling points of this work are concise chapters with subheadings for easy access and the use of examples taken from my publications and presentations.

Book Length
The length will be 60,000–70,000 words, including chapter endnotes and bibliographic references according to *The Chicago Manual of Style*. The manuscript, endnotes, and references will be structured in the format of the proposed Redwood Guides to Indexing.

Proposed Table of Contents

Introduction
1. The Structure of an Index
2. A Brief History of American and European Indexing
3. Indexing a Journal
4. Indexing a Book
5. Indexing a Series
6. Library Indexing

Decisions, decisions! What to include
1. I Liked This Index Because It Was Interesting
2. I Liked This Index Because It Was Comprehensive
3. I Liked This Index Because the Indexer Knew the Subject

Don't Bore Yourself
1. Cross-Indexing: When to Stop
2. Library Systems
3. Topic Choices

Appendix I: Significant Words and Phrases and the Importance of the Use of Appropriate Words

Special Features
I plan appendices for further explanations or references that may not fit in with the chapters.

Author Information
I have been a professional indexer for 31 years. I am a specialist in the Library of Congress and Dewey systems and was the first index librarian at the Nome Athenaeum, past chair of the Indexing Center at the headquarters Word Processing Center in Melbourne, Australia. I have produced 21 publications and presentations in the United States and Australia. Of note are the following:

"The Mobile Indexer" and "The Story of an Athenaeum Numberer," in *Eccentric Categories*. McCard Publishers, 2008.
"My Career in International Indexing," presentation to the Bibliographic Women's Club, November 20, 2007, Providence, RI.
"Indexing issues of Jamaica and Wales," presentation to The Colloquium on Development, Gregynog Hall, Newtown, Wales, May 2001.
"Multiple Careers in Indexing," *Indexing Trends*. vol. 2, no. 3. June 2001

Web Pages
"The Nome Athenaeum," www.nomeathenaeum.com.
Nylorac Sivad, *Access Guide*. accessguidecardiff-online.blog.com.

I was included in *Who's Who in Indexing: 1992–1993*. My community service has included membership in the Advisory Committee to the Governor's Commission on Indexing (Rhode Island) 1987–1988 and work as a spokesperson for the Indexing Society (Rhode Island) 1977–1985.

My employment history encompasses 20 years of research, project development, and implementation, as well as publications and presentations as an indexer since 1996 and a generic researcher from 1988 to 1996. I have facilitated research in projects and have been an indexer for publishers including Specific Bungalow and Dolphin Publications. I have obtained information on pollutant parameters in California; researched and written international reports on indexing in Europe; reported on library research and other conditions in the United Kingdom; and initiated Internet access in organizations in Nome, Alaska, and Melbourne, Australia.

A CV with a publications/presentations list is attached.

Proposed Delivery Date
July 31, 2009

Article proposals follow a form that is included in calls for submissions for magazines, journals, and anthologies. A standard form includes the title, an outline of the subject, and the prospective author's biographical sketch and resume with an emphasis on the author's credentials to write the article, particularly for a nonfiction work. General word counts are usually provided by the editor of the publication, but the author may include it in the proposal. Specific requirements for query letters or e-mails, proposals, and manuscript submissions are typically included on the Web pages of agents and publishers.

SURVEYS

Research surveys can be appropriate and fairly accurate ways to collect information. They are used to collect data for many reasons and to analyze categories of data ranging from opinions to empirical data about populations. Surveys are developed and used by people in many fields. The training for survey design includes courses in statistical analysis, to plot mathematical variations in data, and research methods. Following are a survey and presentation that I conducted in 1998 under the auspices of the Jamaica Council for Persons with Disabilities. Surveys are tools of persuasion because they present data that back up the surveyors' points and conclusions. The following survey was conducted for The Jamaica Council for Persons with Disabilities. I obtained the results below by visiting the agencies and talking to the directors and employees after getting their permission to include each agencies' data in the survey. The results persuaded the agency directors to form a national coalition.

The Jamaica Coalition on Persons with Disability/Report on Agencies

By Carolyn Davis, who conducted the survey and presented the findings in April 1999 to the committee that became the Jamaica Coalition on Disability.

Report

Surveys and interviews are in progress nationwide regarding the actual numbers of persons with disabilities who are clients of agencies that provide rehabilitation, vocational, and/ or educational services. This type of non-medical quantitative and qualitative survey is unprecedented in Jamaica. In addition to determining the number of people in Jamaica who are listed in programs, the surveys and interviews are intended to determine the challenges faced by the service providers and the challenges faced by the clients in accessing the services.

The agencies that have been interviewed to date are listed on page 111.

The interviews are conducted in person or by telephone. Agencies to be contacted in the near future include Goodwill, and some agencies that provide services to clients who are hearing impaired. Interviews are pending with the Combined Disabilities Association and the Caribbean Child Development Centre at University of the West Indies. Care is taken to try not to provide redundant information. The three components in this survey necessitate that more than one agency providing similar services be included, for instance, those focused on people who are hearing impaired and physically disabled.

These numbers reflect only those who are affiliated with the agencies. The numbers do not indicate those people who do not participate in any agency services or benefits.

Approximately 99 percent of the agencies surveyed are in desperate need of increased funding and trained long-term staff. As the agencies have identified, one will lead to the other. The funding problems are profound. For example, although some of the agencies surveyed have had word processors and printers donated to them, items such as replacement print cartridges and other maintenance items are too expensive, necessitating sparing use of the word processor or printer. Organizations such as 3D, the National Children's Home, STEP Centre, and the Clarendon Group for the Disabled use volunteer help full time and depend on funding in part from international organizations such as the United Nations and foreign governments, primarily the European Union, Japan, Canada, and the United States.

Limited access to transportation, embarrassment, and misunderstanding, among other factors, deter parents and other caregivers from seeking help for their disabled children/charges. Many children's disabilities become more serious because appropriate medical evaluation and treatment are denied to them. For example, children with hydrocephalus are unable

Survey of Disability Support Agencies in Jamaica, 1998

Agency	Number by Gender			Notes
	Male	Female	Total	
Jamaica Association for the Deaf	N/A*	N/A	10,000	
The STEP Centre	8	7	15	
National Children's Home	N/A	N/A	34	
Salvation Army School for the Blind	N/A	N/A	115	
Jamaica Society for the Blind	N/A	N/A	N/A	
Clarendon Group for the Disabled Approximately	N/A	N/A	300	
School of Hope / Jamaica Association for Mentally Handicapped Children	N/A	N/A	1,250	
St. Hugh's Prep	3	7	10	Waiting list
Abilities Foundation	28	28	56	
Mustard Seed/JA Association for Children with Learning Disabilities	37	78	115	
Christian Deaf Fellowship Centre	26	17	43	
Caribbean Christian Centre for the Deaf	N/A*	N/A	N/A	
Maranatha School for the Deaf	25	15	40	
Mico Care Centre	N/A	N/A	N/A	
Mona Rehabilitation Centre	N/A	N/A	559	
Private Voluntary Organisation/Special Olympics	N/A	N/A	N/A	
Kiddies Nursery and Learning Centre	N/A	N/A	0	None enrolled
Deeds Industries	18	6	24	
Special Education Unit, Ministry of Education	N/A	N/A	N/A	
Voluntary Social Services	2	9	11	

*N/A = not available.

to have the appropriate surgery for shunting, those with diseases of the endocrine system often become disabled for want of diagnosis and appropriate medications, and those who appear to have glaucoma or cataracts are untreated. Roughly 85 percent of all people with disabilities who are registered with agencies have not been evaluated by a physician. We can guess that those who are not registered with any agency, an estimated 15 percent of the population of Jamaica, have not been evaluated by a physician.

People with disabilities can be helped to lead more normal, inclusive lives via the education of parents, caregivers, and the rest of society. Public awareness can be increased via the use of the media. (The International Year of the Disabled and Disabilities Week are examples of this.) Through the media and presentations in communities, more people can be educated about the benefits of prenatal and other medical care to prevent birth injuries and illnesses, and appropriate care and rehabilitation when a disability occurs. Proper treatment requires a higher budgetary priority, but the initial investment allows more persons with disabilities to lead normal lives at home and in the workplace.[10]

THE RESUME

A resume is a standard instrument of persuasion in a professional setting. There are many ways to structure a resume, but the standard elements include dates, job titles and responsibilities, and companies' names. The names of references and the text of a particularly good reference letter can be included at the end.

In *Resume Writing and Interviewing Techniques That Work*, Robert R. Newlen writes,

> Every individual, as well as prospective employer, is different, . . . resume writing is not one-size-fits-all. Your experience, education, accomplishments, skills, and job objectives are unique. But how do you create a resume that is tailored to your unique experience as well as the needs of your prospective employer? . . . But resume substance won't be our only concern. We will also carefully examine the *look* of the resume. Is it visually appealing? Does it jump out at your potential employer?
> . . . [R]emember that the resume is *you*.[11]

Additionally, a resume is a persuasive writing tool. You use it to persuade someone to interview you for a job. If you are trying to get an article, essay, or a book published, you use it to persuade editors to pay attention to your work.

Summary of Qualifications

Write one or two paragraphs of your skills and work experiences. Include any experiences that demonstrate particular skills or accomplishments, for example,

I managed a budget of $200,000.

Work Experience

List the work that is specific to the position you are applying for. For example, for a research position, see the following work experience.

2009–2006: CONSULTANT IN RESEARCH AND AUTHOR. SEE PUBLICATIONS AND PRESENTATIONS

- Develop and present firsthand information on ways and means of physical and psychological access in libraries for people who have disabilities. Scheduled to teach a continuing education course for librarians regarding their experiences with the Americans with Disabilities Act of 1990.

VOLUNTEER POSITIONS

List any positions that relate to the work that you seek and describe them. For example,

2009-2008: Brightridge Animal Shelter
Care provider: responsible for exercising, cleaning, and playing with 20 dogs

Honors and Awards

List honors and awards as appropriate. For example:

Who's Who in the South and Southwest 1992–1993.
The Edward J. French Award 1978.

Community Service

List any groups you have belonged to that are involved in community work, or any work that you have done in public service. For example,

2010–2009: UNITED WAY OF MASSACHUSETTS. MEMBER, EXECUTIVE DIRECTOR SEARCH COMMITTEE.

Member of a team that reviewed resumes and interviewed candidates.

Education

List your schools, degrees and certifications awarded and the years.

SIMMONS COLLEGE: Boston, MA. MS in Library and Information Science. Graduated 1996.

UNIVERSITY OF WALES: Aberystwyth. Certificate in Library Technology. 1995.

RHODE ISLAND COLLEGE: Providence, RI. BA in Geography. Graduated 1988.

OTHER PROGRAMS: In addition to the degrees, I have approximately 48 credits in an undergraduate International Relations program at Brown University, Providence, Rhode Island. I have many credits in the MS program at the Institute of Conflict Analysis and Resolution at George Mason University, including an internship at the Centre for the Study of Conflict at the University of Coleraine, Northern Ireland.

Memberships

List any groups you belong to. For example,

American Library Association
Women's Archive of Wales: Executive Board Member, 2007–2001

Publications and Presentations

List any publications and presentations as appropriate. For example,
"Do You Want to Be an Anthologist?" and "The Librarian and Researcher Who Is Disabled," in *Writing and Publishing: The Librarian's Handbook*, ed. Carol Smallwood. Chicago: American Library Association. Expected 2009.

PICTURES

Whether visual or a spoken description, pictures can enhance and punctuate written reports and other persuasive material. When your readership visualizes your subject, it becomes more real and more persuasive. As you are planning your written material, check with your teacher, supervisor, or editor to discover if pictures are acceptable and, if so, in which formats. Publications have guidelines for what formats of illustrations or photographs they will accept.

Unusual Situations

One reason you may be asked to present a report or publish an essay or article is that you have had particular experience in a distinct or unusual situation. Following is a sample of my history as a researcher of laws and policies concerning people with disabilities.

> The treatments and understanding of the human body in the 1960s were fairly primitive by 21st century standards, to a considerable degree because technology had not advanced enough to enable people to observe as much of the function of living bodies as they do today. However, attitudes regarding the practice of rehabilitative treatments were changing. Particularly notable to me in the early seventies was the vast improvement in New York from 1960s Rhode Island. That was a prerequisite for the tidal wave of information, new treatments, patient participation, and the multitude of possibilities that were to manifest during the next thirty years and beyond.[12]

Since age 12, I have been asked to speak to people in a variety of settings about my functioning with a disability. In the past 20 years, my presentations and publications about my personal experiences have changed to those of legislative examples concerning people in the United States, Jamaica, and Britain who are disabled. Following is another example of a proposal I was asked to submit to the Office of Library and Information Services in January 2009 regarding a presentation on ADA and Section 504.

INTRODUCTION
This is an outline of a presentation and an explanation of the relevant portions of the Americans with Disabilities Act and Section 504 as they relate to libraries. The workshop will include the reasons that librarians and library staff should be familiar with the specifics of the sections of these laws and how to maintain ADA standards in their workplaces.

SCOPE AND PURPOSE
I plan to present examples of varieties of obstacles and challenges to patrons with disabilities, including computer access and use, and ways to deal with them. Additionally, I will present a brief analysis of the history of and reasons for acts and how they apply to research settings and libraries.

AUDIENCE
The audience will be Rhode Island librarians and other library employees in the state.

MATERIALS

The relevant sections and examples of the ADA and Section 504, and examples of ways libraries are implementing and sustaining them will be projected and distributed to the audience.

CONCLUSION

Discussions with the audience about the sections of the laws, followed by question, answer, and example time.

THE HALO EFFECT

I know of a man whose main claim to fame is self-promotion. Although he carries many titles, the actual work that is credited to him is done by assistant administrators and vice chairs of committees. He has become nationally recognized in his country through the work of his assistants, with no an acknowledgment by him of the work of these loyal, self-effacing people. One time, when he was set to assume the chairmanship of an organization that would ensure additional kudos and funding for him, and a lot of extra work for the vice chair, I sought to warn the woman. After I told her that the man's chairmanship would ensure that it would be *she* who, unheralded, would do the real work, she replied almost blissfully that she wouldn't mind, as long as she would be able to work with the man.

"My goodness," I thought. "The old con artist's strategy worked—on this woman, anyway." As I was about to remonstrate with her that the light of her endeavors would not only be hidden, but completely snuffed out, as he walked over her to grab the credit that belonged to her, another way of reasoning came to me. The lazy, credit-grabbing man had a significant role in the new organization, although it was not the one he would have described. His role was to inspire the people who would do the work. By attracting the media he would raise public support for the organization and attract funding, which the organization needed.

Self-promotion has its merits, and, although the shameless self-promoters who prosper solely as the real workers toil without thanks ought to be identified as the exploiters that they are, more discreet and inclusive forms of self-promotion can be marvelous vehicles of persuasion, as the resume and professional profile attest.

This takes us back to the beginning, and ultimately brings us back to money. If you are identified with an organization or cause, and you are believed and well liked by those who work with you and promote you, you can be a significant asset to your group, whatever your function is. Nevertheless, be sure to acknowledge others' work and beware of alienating people: what we are aiming for is the constructive use of public relations, not your lonely, ruthless climb to fame and wealth. An important strategy in mediation and coalition or consensus building is to identify what is actually happening. This process involves peeling away the extraneous material, usually after a considerable amount of talking, so each party may identify what the real issues are in a situation. A similar strategy is used in persuasive writing in which the real issues of a situation are identified.

DEVELOP STRATEGIES

Good public relations strategies are always useful and often necessary. As illustrated in the example of the man whose main contribution to the organization of which he was the titular leader was self promotion, a positive image can attract good workers to your cause, as well as the motivation to achieve goals, recognition, funding, and ultimately success.

In addition to public relations, work strategies, and realistic goals to be met in an appropriate time frame, add to the clarity of the vision and enhance motivation. The March of Dimes, an organization of national importance that was founded by Franklin Delano Roosevelt to raise money to combat polio, provides a profound example of the success of persuasion through public relations. In the late 1930s and 1940s, under the auspices of The March of Dimes' chairperson Basil O'Connor, movie theaters showed film clips of people hospitalized with the disease. Another film clip portrayed polio anthropomorphized as a menacing presence with an even more menacing voice. The shadowy presence was "not prejudiced, [by race, creed, or gender]" and "loved . . . little children."[13] After these frightening flicks, ushers walked down the aisles with receptacles to collect money to support March of Dimes research and development of treatments and prevention of the disease. These and other national efforts culminated in the development of vaccines by Jonas Salk and Albert Sabin, and ultimately, the eradication of polio in The United States.

Following are some examples of the strategies used by Frances Perkins, Franklin Roosevelt's secretary of labor, throughout her career. A persuasive person in her own right, New Yorker Perkins advanced politically in her state by working out who in the corrupt Tammany Hall administration was reasonably reliable and willing to work and cultivating their patronage. Eventually that networking enabled her to join Theodore Roosevelt's staff, and ultimately the administration of Theodore Roosevelt's nephew-in-law, Franklin.[14]

Perkins' examples emphasize the importance of learning the details of a situation in which persuasion can be used effectively.

Frances Perkins became a social worker and political activist. Her experiences informed her social awareness. Her writing of the time says something of her own and President Franklin Roosevelt's perceptions.

The following example is quite persuasive in its hoped-for transition to a different perspective about "the poor" by people of middle and upper incomes in the United States.

> Foremost was the idea that poverty is preventable, that poverty is destructive, wasteful, demoralizing, and that poverty in the midst of potential plenty is morally unacceptable in a Christian and democratic society. One began to see the "poor" as people, with hopes, fears, virtues, and vices, as fellow citizens who were part of the fabric of American life instead of as a depressed class who would be always with us.[15]

As secretary of labor for President Franklin Roosevelt from 1933 to 1945, Perkins developed some plans for economic aid to people who were unemployed and elderly. She also recommended a structure to improve the quality of life for wage earners.

> I proposed immediate federal aid to the states for direct unemployment relief, an extensive program of public works, a study and an approach to the establishment by federal law of minimum wages, maximum hours, true unemployment and old-age insurance, abolition of child labor, and the creation of a federal employment service.[16]

In her biography of Roosevelt, Perkins wrote:

> In one of my conversations with the President in March 1933, he brought up the idea that became the Civilian Conservation Corps. Roosevelt loved trees and hated to see them cut and not replaced. It was natural for him to wish to put large numbers of the unemployed to repairing such devastation. His enthusiasm for this project, which was really all his own, led him to some exaggeration of what could be accomplished. He saw it big. He thought any man or boy would rejoice to leave the city and work in the woods.
>
> It was characteristic of him that he conceived the project, boldly rushed it through, and happily left it to others to worry about the details. And there were some difficult details. . . .
>
> The attitude of the trade unions had to be considered. They were disturbed about this program, which they feared would put all workers under a "dollar a day" regimentation merely because they were unemployed.[17]

People who truly want to persuade must deal with details. President Roosevelt, as all U.S. presidents, however, "persuaded" his staff to work out the details of his plans by his implicit threat power. He could fire them if they did not follow his orders. Special interest groups required different handling from the president's employees. Their fears needed to be addressed, or they might have persuaded their members not to have voted for the president at the next election. The unions and other groups had threat power over the president.

All politicians use persuasion to lead and coerce in many ways and on many levels. During the decades following World War II, economic prosperity prompted such researchers as Carl I. Hovland of Yale University to study the psychology of persuasion. Building on Hovland's work, scholars at business schools and other institutions further explored methods for reaching agreement. On a less theoretical level, politicians, including Harry S. Truman, recognized the power that comes from influencing people. This research continued during the 1970s and 1980s, and leading business schools increasingly made the art of persuasion part of their coursework. The study of persuasion continues today, both in psychology programs and in business schools around the country.[18]

Religious documents are another example of highly persuasive material. The following is a sermon delivered by Elizabeth Vincent, at the time the interim associate minister at Newman Church in Rumford, Rhode Island.[19] Look at the building of a persuasive argument in the text. In these passages, Vincent begins by using personal examples, and then expands to the universal.

THE IMAGE OF GOD

The greatest praise that we can offer to God is our service to one another.

The "Wii"—this past Christmas I was introduced to the "Wii," and judging from the reported sales of the game, many of you may have been as well. What is it? Well, I describe it as a family computer sport. It hooks up to your television and allows you to engage in a wide variety of sports and games right in your living room. Now, I am not certain if it is easier to accept, "Honey, I'm off to play 18 at the club," or "Honey, we're going to play 18" (and the living room is off limits for the next two hours). Of course, you, the person, are not really playing golf—or racing motorbikes—you create this little image of you—an avatar called a "Mii."

Creating the "Mii" is a game in itself. You pick a body shape that best represents you (or your alter ego), you pick the hair color (you want), hair style, eyes, lips, height, etc. You even pick the "favorite color," which your "Mii" quickly dons.

As I was creating my "Mii," the thought passed through my mind, "I wonder if this is what it is like to be God?" Here I am creating a little being. Quickly, it hit me that I was actually picking from a laundry list of alternative looks and colors. So, maybe not me, but the creator of that laundry list is like God—a software programmer! Well, maybe it is more likely that the concept designer is more like God. The question kept spinning in my mind until the "god" of "Mii" was a remote, hugely expansive, and very powerful brain—not the very involved and laughing "ME" (*point to self*), who was sharing time with my family in the living room.

The empowerment of electronics! The software developer becomes a God-like being who, through the magic of software, enables a person to create an alter-ego from a set of prescribed categories.

From this personal musing about creating beings in cyberspace, Reverend Vincent then moves from personal to larger settings:

God—who is he—*she*—*it*—*them*? What is God? Where is God? Of course, I am most certainly not the first person to ask these questions—the search for answers is the backbone of scripture.

This morning's scripture reading from the Book of Isaiah, Chapter 40, seeks to describe God to the Israelites as they return to Jerusalem from their exile in Babylonia. According to Old Testament scholars, the previous 39 chapters were written before the exile. Warnings and exhortations leap off the pages. Yet, Chapter 40 begins with the words, "Comfort, O comfort my people, says your God. Speak tenderly to Jerusalem . . ." This is followed in verse 11 with the description of God as a gentle shepherd. We feel nurtured, cared for, and loved by a close-by presence. However, a mere 10 verses later we are asked:

Have you not known? Have you not heard? Has it not been told you from the beginning? Have you not understood from the foundations of the earth?

The answer given is:

It is he who sits above the circle of the earth, and its inhabitants are like grasshoppers . . .

Suddenly, God is very powerful and very remote. There is a phrase that the God described here is sitting so far above us that even the "uncles" look like "ants."

Humor and punning, used sparingly, are marvelous vehicles for teaching a lesson and making a point. Reverend Vincent makes comparisons repeatedly between human and divine relationships. In these she is preparing a lesson that she will "bring home" in the next few paragraphs.

It is understandable that our praise, our worship, of this powerful and very remote God is full of words of awe and majesty. I am reminded of a fairly popular, and very uplifting, praise song:

"Our God is an awesome God, He reigns from heaven above, our God is an awesome God."

Yet is this really what this scripture is telling us? The passage continues this pattern of questions and responses. In verse 23 we are asked, "who stretches out the heavens like a curtain, . . . who brings princes to naught, and makes the rulers of the earth as nothing?" The response of verse 24 reminds us of just how tenuous and brief is our life. In verse 25 we are asked, "To whom then will you compare me?" We are then reminded of God's mighty power; and finally, we are asked why it is that we doubt God's continuing interest in us—God's capacity to care about us. The next verses assure us of God's continuing presence, God's continuing support of us, even when we fall to the ground spent, beyond weary.

Now this could be understood to be saying, "Look at me, I am huge, I am so powerful, so far above you, that all you may do is grovel in the dirt waiting for my directions, my approval," until we recall that these verses follow God's command to the Israelite peoples to "Cry out" (verse 6) from a high mountain, "lift up your voice with strength" and say to all "Here is your God!"(verse 9). The command is there—we are to proclaim our God to the world.

Now, I will share with you that there have been times in my life when I have screamed out, "God, what do you want me to do? Tell me—and because I seem to be so dense—smack me over the head with a 2 × 4 until I hear you." Sure enough, I usually got a smack in the head. However, the smack was not from God, the smack came as a result of not getting up and "proclaiming" my God to the world.

"And what does that mean?" you might ask. It does bring to mind an image of a "John the Baptist," an "Elijah," or possibly a street-corner evangelist. It brings to mind the stadiums filled with people—their hands held high, their faces radiant with God's love, their voices strong and confident as songs praising a mighty and powerful God fill their bodies with exuberant joy for our God. Certainly this is to "proclaim" God. Yet, this is the God of the "way up there"—how do we "proclaim" the shepherd who feeds, gathers, carries, and leads us?

Our gospel lesson is from Mark—the succinct, terse, "just give me the facts, ma'am" gospel. The reading appears as three, brief, seemingly unconnected scenes from the beginning of Jesus' public ministry. Loosely, they are structured as follows:

Scene one: (1) Jesus enters the house of Simon and Andrew to find Simon's mother-in-law in bed with a fever. (2) Jesus takes her hand thereby lifting her up. (3) The fever departs. (4) She begins to serve them.

Scene two: (1) The sick and possessed gather at the door. (2) Jesus cures the ill and possessed. (3) Jesus commands of the demons anonymity.

Scene three: (1) Jesus goes out alone to pray. (2) His disciples hunt for him and find him. (3) They "reprimand" him for leaving the crowds who want more healing. (4) Jesus suggests that they go to the neighboring towns to "proclaim the message." (5) Jesus reminds his disciples that proclamation is what he came "out" to do.

Now, are these little vignettes truly unconnected? In both scenes one and two there is healing. In the first, the mother-in-law gets up and life continues as usual. This used to seem a little convenient to me—the men are hungry, Jesus heals the mother-in-law, and she feeds them. However, in the second scene, the demons are told to be quiet, but the town's people run around telling people about the miracle healings and then expect more miracles. Their focus and that of the disciples is on the miracles. In the third scene, we actually get the lesson—"I came out to proclaim the message, not to amaze people with miracles." Sound a little familiar?

In the Isaiah reading the miraculous, amazing God is described to the Israelites in a series of rhetorical questions. The command is to "proclaim God," the God who feeds, gathers, and gently nurtures. In Mark, the crowds clamored for more and more miracles; Simon's mother-in-law simply began to serve—to *wait* on those around her. It was through her service she proclaimed the miracle of her healing. She proclaimed her God.

The final verse of Isaiah 40 reads:

*But those who **wait** for the Lord shall renew their strength, they shall mount up with wings like eagles, they shall run and not be weary, they shall walk and not faint.*

The word "wait" is from a Hebrew root word that connects food—nourishment—with the waiting. It is a word that suggests action as a result of God's blessings. It is the act of proclaiming the miracle of God's presence in the midst of everyday life. It is the act of serving others to the glory of God.

Reverend Vincent then makes a transition from the examples of service in Isaiah to examples of service in our daily lives. She offers some fine examples of persuasion: personal observation, comparison, and interpretation from the personal to the larger example, and back from the biblical metaphor to the personal example.

We stand in the glorious reach of God's creation—we close our eyes, lift our faces, feel God's love embrace our being—and our soul soars to the heights of eternal hope. Stand in that glowing and lofty, unencumbered place, and rest in the arms of God even if for only one moment in a day—then open your eyes, smile and join the world in newness, peace, and service. Amen.

From Reverend Vincent's sermon and my interpretation of it, let us now move to another structure that focuses on another minister in a previous era. The late Reverend Dr. Augustus Sidney Lovett Jr. was born in Boston, Massachusetts, in 1890. Lovett served as minister of the Mount Vernon Congregational Church in Boston for 13 years, and from 1932 to 1958 he served as chaplain of Yale University. The next year Lovett was named executive vice president of "Yale-in-China," which became known as Yale-China.[20]

The patriarch of two subsequent generations of ministering Lovetts, Reverend Lovett, called "Uncle Sid," during his tenure in New Haven, wrote an inspiring and humorous summary of his perception of his life and faith in a collection for Yale University of some of his work and others' remembrances of him.

To sum up, I can say with the Psalmist that "the lines are fallen unto me in pleasant places." I rejoice in the achievements of my three successors—the late Quincy Porter, John Hershey, and William Sloane Coffin. The last two are friends from my undergraduate days. I miss earlier contact with students. But with age comes a preference to listen rather than to talk. One tends to travel light with respect to certainties about ultimate things. Yet in my kitbag is the conviction that the human pilgrimage will not end in any bleak desert of despair. Rather, it moves, however slowly, toward the completion of all that is now partial or fragmentary in God, from Whom we have come forth and unto Whom we are set to return.

To avoid misrepresentation, I have written my own epitaph with a verbal acknowledgement to a memorable Englishman (Sir Winston Churchill, Prime Minister of the United Kingdom, 1940–'45, 1951–'55), "Never has anyone endowed with so few natural gifts gotten away with so much."[21]

In the preceding passage, Reverend Lovett's acknowledgments, nostalgia, and statement of faith are leavened by his self-effacing quotation at the end. It is a nice lesson in the art and craft of writing about oneself: a little humor can underscore an important message instead of detracting from it.

A LITTLE MORE ABOUT PRESENTATIONS

When preparing a presentation, think of ways to involve your audience at many points. Its members' understanding and engagement in the topic increase everyone's receptiveness, even the speaker's. Increased receptiveness helps to increase the audience's ability and willingness to incorporate the speaker's point of view to its own, and during a personal presentation, a speaker has options—through eye contact, humor, expressions of understanding, and the ability to respond to the audience immediately and adjust the speech appropriately—that a writer has not, because a written presentation is neither immediate nor presented personally. Of course, the presenter's receptiveness to the audience has a considerable impact on the success of presenter–audience interaction. The presenter needs to be receptive to the format of the presentation and to the audience. Sometimes it may takes some minutes, or even an hour or so of warm-up before constructive interaction occurs. As in any relationship, the relationship has to develop. A good strategy is to plan some strategies for interaction and then, during the presentation, to gauge when these strategies are appropriate to initiate.

In *Through Charley's Door*, Emily Kimbrough's account of her employment during the 1920s at Marshall Field's department store, Kimbrough wrote of the tremendous influence that the then head buyer of the store's book department had on the reading preferences of people in the United States. The buyer had this persuasive position because she sold more books than any other retailer.[22]

Kimbrough gives an example of this power retailer's position. *The Prairie Years*, a volume of Carl Sandburg's biography of Abraham Lincoln, was intended as a prestige work with a significantly limited market. The woman ordered 1,000 copies of the book for Marshall Field's. Other retailers, knowing of her abilities to sense and create sales, ordered proportionally for their stores, and Sandburg became a bestselling author.[23]

There is a dark side to massive media power, of which Senator Joseph McCarthy's drunken bids for attention in the late 1940s and early 1950s and Adolf Hitler's election as chancellor of Germany in 1933 are but two of the menacing examples: what if the power of the media is set against you because you happen at a particular time to belong to a group that is out of favor?

SPREAD THE WORD

A Persuasive Cover Letter

A cover letter usually accompanies a resume in a job interview and is meant to influence a prospective employer that you are qualified for the job and are an appropriate candidate to interview. You present an interesting picture of yourself as you explain why your qualifications suit the position.

Following is a fictitious letter from an environmental policy advocate to a nonprofit organization. Notice that specific dates are not mentioned because the dates, places, and descriptions of the applicant's employment have been listed in the resume. The structure of the letter is similar to a five-paragraph essay. The first sentence states the position for which the candidate is applying. Subsequent paragraphs emphasize the applicant's education and responsibilities: in this case, they are the facts that back up the application. The final paragraph summarizes why the applicant is a good choice for the position.

Dear _____ ,

This letter is to apply for the position of Project Coordinator of the Southwest Division for The Environment First.

I was raised in Denver, Colorado, and became a research assistant to Avak Havertian, PhD, prior to receiving my PhD in Environmental Management from The University of California at Los Angeles. Since then I have worked in a variety of positions as a manager, supervisor, and advocate in nonprofit agencies.

(Note that in all of the following job descriptions the applicant mentions specific tasks. In the first example, the candidate mentions a project's sustainable development [the project still exists]. The other descriptions include the number of people the candidate supervised, the budgets, and the amount of money saved.

In the concluding paragraph, the applicant mentions familiarity with the organization's goals and specific people known.)

> As a Peace Corps Volunteer in Haiti, I facilitated the construction of a waste recycling center near Port-au-Prince. Still in operation, the center recycles 15 tons of paper and 10 tons of tin and aluminum annually.
>
> After my Peace Corps service, I became an assistant Media Coordinator for the Environmental Protection Agency where I was responsible for press releases and interviews. During my tenure there, I issued statements to the press, chaired conferences concerning the impact of court decisions on national laws and policies, and was responsible for a staff of 16.
>
> As Director of Project Earth in Butte, Montana, I supervised a staff of 18 and a budget of $600,000. I facilitated a recycling program that processed eight tons of metal waste per month. This metal was recycled in Butte into reusable beverage containers, and brought the amount of metal waste in Butte down from 45% to 25%, at an estimated savings to the city of $2,350,000 annually and a considerable benefit to the environment.
>
> My background in sustainable development, administration, budget supervision, and public relations is well suited to the position of Project Manager. I am very familiar with The Environment First's work setting up recycling centers in developing nations. Two people from my Peace Corps group, Emanuel Lima and Shaney Yolana, are project coordinators.
>
> Thank you for your consideration.

The following essay was developed from research conducted on colonization ethics from the early modern European time, approximately 1492–1776, or from the time of Columbus's expeditions to the West Indies to the American Revolution. Great questions are posed from time to time about the influence of European transatlantic exploration from the 15th to the 19th centuries: What if everyone had stayed home? What if people hadn't felt the concurrent need as they were exploring to claim for European monarchs land that was already occupied? What were the ethics of colonization? The essay uses biographical facts about Christopher Columbus and Western European history of the early modern time (1450–1775) to explain the reasons for colonization and why it was supported by European society. This essay doesn't seek to persuade the reader that the colonizing nations were right to colonize, but to explain how the participating nations justified colonization at the time and persuaded others to participate.

Look at the motivating factors of the 15th–19th centuries. Have the motivating factors of interest groups today changed in 400 years? What are some of our motivating factors for work in other countries that we perceive or claim to be philanthropic today? In what ways might philanthropic work be harmful to people of other cultures? How do we persuade everyone to participate?

Christopher Columbus was part of a large group of men who from the 15th to the 20th centuries developed ways to gather resources for their sponsors, and were encouraged not only in their acquisitions of material wealth by European royalty and business interests, but in their spreading Christianity to other lands.[24]

From the 15th century through the next 400 years, Western Europeans felt an "obligation" to bring their civilization and religious beliefs to other lands. Moral obligation is a theme that is repeated continuously throughout history and continues to this day to be used to justify outside intervention in many sociopolitical events. Slavery and indentured servitude were European traditions of long-standing. As the Europeans brought their cultures to the West Indies, they brought paternalism and class distinction, with little need or practice to analyze the moral right or wrong of impressing people into a work and value system about which the laborers had little say, and through which they were subjected to personal violation, disease, and genocide.[25]

The Western Europeans had the capital, muscle, and ability in those who were willing to take part, for transoceanic travel and battle, and, as has also happened repeatedly throughout history, they had the means to spread their culture and religion. The philosophy of "might makes right" has been debated many times, but in the late Middle Ages and early modern period it was a leading factor in the development of colonies, especially since the spread of Christianity was a key issue.[26]

By European standards of the late Middle Ages and on to the modern period, "duty" was a rallying cry in colonization. An explorer had a duty to his sovereign, his society, and God. To explore and acquire new lands was truly a holy and national mission for the good of everyone, it was believed. The missions and often the men involved in them were respected for the work that colonizing was.[27] There are similarities to space exploration during the Cold War and philanthropic work abroad by U.S. government agencies today. The ethics of the 400 years of the practice, then, supported it as good.

People are inclined to react to situations from the perspectives of their own times. Although the time frame doesn't affect the impact of an action, for instance, colonizers exploited people and resources horribly, it is necessary to look at the historical perspective of a situation to understand the motivation behind actions.

THE POSITIVE OUTCOME OF A STORY: THREE WISE WOMEN FROM THE EAST

Overcoming prejudice has an impact that is highly persuasive. This is an example of my worldview expanding through an unusual encounter. I wrote it as an example of persuasion through reporting an incident, similar to the reporting in the letter about the children's home in Jamaica at the beginning of this chapter.

We all have "clenches" to face. One of mine is a fortunately rare occurrence during which, while I'm lying on my stomach during an exercise, the muscles of my arm contract, which in turn affects my lower and sometimes upper back muscles similarly. The effect is not unlike that of labor pains, with rhythmic, painful contractions, except that I can be rendered nearly immobile with nothing as rewarding as a baby to anticipate. Relief comes when I am turned over on my back and my muscles can move as they are inclined.

One of these episodes happened when I was a research associate in history at the University of Wales at Cardiff. I was on my bed in a dormitory, feeling badly, painfully, stuck. After about a half-hour, another research candidate came down the hall. Fortunately, the woman had excellent hearing and perception. She heard and understood when I called softly and hoarsely, " Becky, I need help. . . . In a clench."

"I'll get someone," she responded, and disappeared in a flash. Approximately two minutes later, three women in conservative Muslim attire came in and, with the precision of a trained ambulance crew, turned me on my back. I had seen them before and had assumed that they were Saudis, as they were usually in the company of women from Saudi Arabia who were medical students. Although I'd not met my three rescuers before, I had spoken with their medical colleagues from time to time: one particularly memorable time to invite them to a dinner party. Their gentle response had been, "We have *dissection* on Tuesdays, and we usually don't eat that day."

The three that I owed my relaxing back to were strangers, however. Although I was not as yet ready to talk, I certainly wanted to listen and learn about them. One told me her name and added, "I'm from Afghanistan." The second said her name with the addition, "From Iraq. You must call us if ever again you get into trouble." As the three wrote down their cell phone numbers and my mind was processing the irony of our home-lands, the third said her name and her country of origin, "From Iran."

I was somewhat weakened from my experience, and the irony that all three of them came from countries in conflict with America left me non-plussed. A weak, fairly emotionless "Oh," escaped my lips, as the Iranian medical student uttered the words that every Iranian of my acquaintance for the past 20-plus years has said: "My family has been here since before the Revolution."

"How many times she has felt obligated to say that to Westerners!" I thought. "Having to justify her presence in Britain, just as I feel so often that I must apologize for the 'wrong moves' of the current United States administration."

I was recuperating fairly quickly by then, and had the presence of mind to say what I truly felt. "You all are wise women from the East," to which they all smiled. "Thank you for taking care of me."

SATIRE

The popularity of the newspaper *Punch* and *Mad* magazine; Gilbert and Sullivan light opera; and the stories of Robert Benchley, E.J. Perelman, and James Thurber just a few of the many publications and a small selection of authors of ironic literature—attest to the popularity of satire. Just as hu-mor is useful in persuasive texts, satire is a marvelous sword with which to persuade (puns can be also). Following is an example of the use of humor to make a point. Since most people enjoy humor, and find it easy to read about mistakes through its medium, it can be an effective means of persuasion.

Dear Reverend X,

This letter is to entreat you to persuade your colleague, Reverend Y, to wear shoes that make some noise. This suggestion is for his protection and that of his congregation. He runs to his tasks with the light, speedy step of Hermes, the Greek messenger god. Although this is commendable and frequently necessary in his daily rounds, his lack of an audible footstep has interesting consequences. Last Sunday I was talking to a three-year-old girl. As I stooped down to retrieve an object I had dropped, I said, "I'll be right back, honey," to be greeted as I sat up, not by the three-year-old, but by the 53-year-old Reverend Y. Even that would not have been so bad, were it not for the fact that his wife is in excellent physical shape and could deck me with half a blow. I am a writer with many deadlines and am inclined to jumpiness.

Many thanks for your prompt attention to this important matter.

Sincerely,

SUMMARY

In the process of providing information to get a point across, there are many choices of the vehicle. Sometimes a "just the facts" approach is appropriate. Sometimes humor, irony, or satire will help to get your point across. Frequently, a human touch helps. The examples in this chapter are provided to demonstrate some choices and their structure. The ways in which you present your points of view should reflect your history, taste, personality, and adaptation to circumstances—such as getting a job or contract.

Think about how to present yourself well and develop your skills for it. Good luck and good work.

NOTES

George Washington Carver, "George Washington Carver Quotes," www.brainyquote.com/quotes/authors/g/george_washington_carver.html.

1. Carolyn Davis, "Strathmore House and Other Issues of Jamaica," included in a letter to "Save the Children," 2006.

2. Ibid., 2.

3. Ibid., 3.

4. Ibid., 4.

5. Ibid., 5. This vignette was part of a collection of writing that formally and informally documented some of the work of some Peace Corps volunteers from 1997 to 1999 and the launch of the Jamaica Coalition on Disability in June 1999.

6. Linda Bridges and William F. Rickenbacker, *The Art of Persuasion: A National Review Rhetoric for Writers* (New York: National Review, 1991), 11.

7. José Ortega y Gasset, *Origen y E pilogo de la Filosofia* (Madrid: Colección, 1980), 89.

8. Joseph Barbato and Danielle S. Furlich, *Writing for a Good Cause: The Complete Guide to Crafting Proposals and Other Persuasive Pieces for Nonprofits* (New York: Fireside, 2000), 87.

9. Ibid., 88.

10. Carolyn Davis, "Access Issues of Jamaica and Wales," presentation to The Colloquium on Development in Gregynog Hall, Newtown, Wales, June 2006.

11. Robert R. Newlen, *Resume Writing and Interviewing Techniques that Work: A How-To-Do-It Manual for Librarians, Number 148* (New York: Neal-Schumann Publishers, 2006), xiv.

12. Carolyn Davis, "A Research Slice of Life," *Writing and Publishing: The Librarian's Handbook* (New York: American Library Association, pending).

13. *American Experience: The Polio Crusade*, www.pbs.org, February 2, 2009.

14. Kirsten Downey, "An Evening with Kirstin Downey, author of *The Woman Behind the New Deal*," presentation at the List Art Center, Brown University, Providence, RI, March 16, 2009.

15. Sparticus Educational, "Frances Perkins," www.spartacus.schoolnet.co.uk/USAR perkins.htm.

16. Ibid.

17. Frances Perkins, *The Roosevelt I Knew* (New York: The Viking Press 1946), 177.

18. "Persuasion: The World's Most Researched Skill," *The Seven Triggers to Yes*, www.seventriggers.com/?p=236.

19. Elizabeth Vincent, "The Image of God," sermon preached at the First Congregational United Church of Christ, Grand Junction, CO, February 8, 2009.

20. Sidney Lovett, "A. Sidney Lovett papers, 1889–1979 (inclusive), MS 1089" (New Haven, CT: Yale University, 1984).

21. William A. Wiedershein, ed., *Uncle Sid of Yale: A Collection of Writings by and about the Late Sidney Lovett, D.D. 1890–1979. Chaplain of Yale University, Theodore Dwight Woolsey Professor of Biblical Literature Emeritus* (New Haven, CT: Yale Alumni Fund, 1981), 2–3.

22. Emily Kimbrough, *Through Charley's Door* (New York: Harper & Brothers Publishers, 1952), 191–192.

23. Ibid., 192.

24. John Marcus Dickey, *Christopher Columbus and his monument Columbia: being a concordance of choice tributes to the great Genoese, his grand discovery, and his greatness of mind and purpose: the testimony of ancient authors, the tributes of modern men, adorned with the sculptures, scenes and portraits of the old world and the new* (Chicago: Rand McNally 1892), www.archive.org/details/christophercolum00dick.

25. Geoffrey Symcox and Blair Sullivan, *Christopher Columbus and the Enterprise of the Indies: A Brief History with Documents: The Bedford Series in History and Culture* (New York: Palgrave MacMillan, 2005), 51–171.

26. Ibid.

27. Ibid.

CHAPTER 5

Resources for the Future

This is an annotated bibliography of the resources that were used to compile this book. The list was relevant and current at the time of publication. Many of the resources refer directly to how-tos and specific examples of persuasive writing. Some sources are biographies of persuasive writers and speakers, and some are persuasive articles and vignettes.

PRINT RESOURCES

Barbato, Joseph. *The Mercifully Brief, Real World Guide to Attracting the Attention Your Cause Deserves*. Medfield, MA: Emerson and Church, 2005. This book *is* brief and geared to writing grant proposals.

Barbato, Joseph, and Danielle S. Furlich. *Writing for a Good Cause: The Complete Guide to Crafting Proposals and Other Persuasive Pieces for Nonprofits*. New York: Fireside, 2000.
    Veteran proposal writers Barbato and Furlich take the reader through the grant writing process by emphasizing the basics, such as, "What is Grant Writing?" and how to propose from strength. They offer solutions for dealing with deadlines, moving "From Notes to Outline" and "From Introduction to Reprise," and finally mailing it in. The topics and processes are presented in realistic, practical ways with humor as a nice leaven.

Bridges, Linda, and William F. Rickenbacker. *The Art of Persuasion: A National Review Rhetoric for Writers*. New York: The National Review, 1991.
    This book is humorous and to the point. It mandates speakers and writers to be entertaining and exciting in their persuasion.

Browning, Beverly A. *Grant Writing for Dummies*. Hoboken, NJ: For Dummies, 2005.

    Beverly Browning is a professional grant writer. This book in the *Dummies* series includes structures and forms of grant writing for a variety of organizations.

Camp, Lindsay. *Can I Change Your Mind?: The Craft and Art of Persuasive Writing*. London: A&C Black, 2007.

    This book is well constructed for many levels of persuasive writing. Author Lindsay Camp has been a copywriter and is a freelancer.

Cunningham, Helen, and Brenda Greene. *Communications Experts at the Fortune 500* . New York: McGraw-Hill, 2002.

    This book offers advice from Fortune 500 companies about constructing e-mail, among other business writing media. "Going with the Flow" and warnings about the limitations of style books are included, as well as tips on effective writing and correspondence manners.

The Essential Writer's Companion: A Concise Guide to Writing Effectively for School, Home, or Office. Boston: Houghton-Mifflin, 1994.

    The Essential Writer's Companion is a comprehensive instruction manual for students, families, and professionals. It includes sections on persuasive writing but is much more broadly focused.

Forsyth, Patrick. *Persuasive Business Writing*. Oxford: How To Books, 2002.

    In this concise guide to successful business writing, chapters cover such topics as overcoming communication problems that obscure clarity. Additionally, the book encouraging learning readers' ways of thinking, setting appropriate objectives, using language appropriately, and, ultimately, securing agreement with readers.

Gasset, José Ortega y. *Origen y Epilogo de la Filosofia* (*The Source and Epilogue of Philosophy*). Mexico City: *Colección*, 1980.

    Ortega's book is an example of the medium's having a great influence on the message. The reader looks for the soul of the author as the author considers the perspectives of the reader.

Gordon, Josh. *Presentations That Change Minds: Strategies to Persuade, Convince and Get Results*. New York: McGraw-Hill, 2006.

The president of Gordon Communications Strategies, Josh Gordon, developed chapters that illustrate how to interest audiences and what presentation traps to avoid.

Lane, Barry. *But How Do You Teach Writing?: A Simple Guide for All Teachers*. Scranton, PA: Scholastic Teaching Resources, 2008.
A humorous instruction manual in the art of teaching persuasive writing to all students. Barry Lane is the author of many cheerfully written books about writing instruction.

Lane, Barry. *51 Wacky We-Search Reports: Face the Facts with Fun*. Shoreham, VT: Discover Writing Press, 2003.
Geared to kindergarten to 12th grade students, this is an exploration of ways to develop the minds and methods of students to help them to think and write well.

Lane, Barry, and Gretchen Bernabei. *Why We Must Run with Scissors: Voice Lessons in Persuasive Writing*. Shoreham, VT: Discover Writing Press, 2001.
This is a collection of lesson plans and exercises for teachers to present to students from 3rd to 12th grades. The book is a humorous and pertinent how-to book that is geared to teaching young students.

McLuhan, Marshall, and Quentin Fiore. *The Medium is the Massage*. Berkeley, CA: Gingko Press, 1967.
This small book describes the ways mass media influences, even brainwashes, the public.

Oettle, Kenneth F. *Making Your Point: A Practical Guide to Persuasive Legal Writing*. New York: ALM Publishing, 2007.
This writing guide is geared to lawyers and paralegals.

Rozakis, Laurie. *Schaum's Quick Guide to Writing Great Research Papers*, 2nd ed. New York: McGraw-Hill, 2007.
As the title states, this book's focus is research papers.

Slagle, Patricia. *Shirley and the Battle of Agincourt: Why It Is So Hard for Students to Write Persuasive Researched Analyses*. Occasional Paper, No. 14. Berkeley, CA: National Center for the Study of Writing and Literacy, 1989.

Slagle uses a representative composite college student named Shirley to demonstrate why many students have difficulty developing arguments that enable them to write persuasive essays. Among the problems that Slagle identifies are students' ignorance of the subject matter, a belief that published sources state "truth" that should not be analyzed or questioned, and a lack of clarity in instructors' and professors' directions for and corrections of essays.

Storey, William Kelleher. *Writing History: A Guide for Students*, 2nd ed. New York: Oxford University Press, 2003.

This book is well constructed and is what it claims. William Kelleher Storey is a professional historian who specializes in colonialism.

Turabian, Kate L. *A Manual for Writers of Research Papers, Theses, and Dissertations: Chicago Style for Students and Researchers*, 7th ed. Chicago: University of Chicago Press, 2007.

Considered the standard guide to the structure of research papers, the manual is a concise and comprehensive guide to academic and professional writing.

ELECTRONIC RESOURCES

Academy of the Arts. "Persuasive Writing." www.orangeusd.k12.ca.us/yorba/persuasive_writing.

This page shows the structure of persuasive essays and suggests choices for opening paragraphs.

Andrade, Heidi Goodrich. "Understanding Rubrics." 1997. MiddleWeb: Exploring Middle School Reform. www.middleweb.com/rubricsHG.html#anchor20268681.

Andrade explains the purpose and function of rubrics, which are evaluation tools designed to help to assess criteria in essays. The article originally appeared in *Educational Leadership*, volume 54, 1997.

Ayres, Ruth, and Stacey Shubitz. "Letters to the Next President: Writing Our Future." Two Writing Teachers. http://twowritingteachers.wordpress.com/2008/08/11/letters-to-the-next-president.

Sponsored by the National Writing Project and Google, this writing and publishing project encouraged high school students to write to the president to express their issues and concerns about the future.

Cabrillo College. "Essays: Putting It All Together." http://www.cabrillo.
edu/services/writingcenter/290/essays.html.
    This site provides step-by-step instructions and examples of exposi-
tory and persuasive writing.

eMINTS National Center. "Writing: Persuasion." www.emints.org/ethemes/
resources/S00000991.shtml.
    Sponsored by the eMINTS National Center, this page is for students
in junior and senior high school.

Essay Start. "Types of Essays: Persuasive Essays." www.essaystart.com/Kinds_
of_Essays/persuasiv_Essays.htm.
    This is a Web page designed for step-by-step instruction in persua-
sive writing and includes many links to lessons and examples.

Gardner, Traci. "traci's list of ten: Ten Persuasive Prompts: Persuasive-
Descriptive." www.tengrrl.com/tens/018.shtml.
    This page is to help high-school students prepare for exit exams, par-
ticularly the Teaching All Secondary Students (TASS) and English II
End of Course standardized tests, on the topics of persuasive-descriptive,
persuasive-classification, how to, classification, and description. Other
categories will be added in the future, and the author asks to be informed
if a topic that she has not included is to be included in the exams.

Kantz, Margaret. "Articles—Self-help, Real life Stories, Persuasive Articles and Persuasive Essays." www.snzeport.com/persuasive-articles.htm.
    These are links to categories and samples of persuasive essays.

Kent School District. "Persuasive Writing Websites." www.kent.k12.wa.us/
curriculum/writing/elem_writing/Bib/Persuasive.htm; and
"Persuasive Writing Websites for Secondary Teachers & Students." www.
kent.k12.wa.us/curriculum/writing/sec_writing/persuasivewritesites.
htm
    These pages contain many links to persuasive writing resources, includ-
ing debates and letters. The feedback is geared to high school students.

Landsberger, Joe. Study Guides and Strategies. www.studygs.net/wrtstr6.
htm.
    This Web site looks at a variety of categories of persuasive writing.
The home page provides definitions, contrasts the major types of essays,

and provides a categorical structure for essay development. Best of all, there is a word game of phrases.

LEO. "Writing a Reaction or Response Essay." http://leo.stcloudstate.edu/acadwrite/reaction.html.

This page from LEO: Literary Education Online recommends prewriting a reaction or response essay using the following questions:

- "How do you feel about what you are reading?"
- "What do you agree or disagree with?"
- "Can you identify with the situation?"
- "What would be the best way to evaluate the story?"

The LEO page provides a chart showing how to structure an essay. The chart suggests key phrases with which to begin sentences. LEO also suggests three ways to frame conclusions: as a restatement of the points of the essay, as a focused overall reaction, or as a prediction.

Lopez, Emy. "Teaching Resource Books for Persuasive Writing." Scholastic. www2.scholastic.com/browse/article.jsp?id=3147.

This page includes book titles for teaching persuasive writing. The content is geared to grades 9–12.

NWP National Writing Project: Improving Writing and Learning in the Nation's Schools. www.nwp.org/cs/public/print/resource_topic/persuasive_writing.

This page features good resources for teachers. Topics include "The Writing Classroom as a Laboratory for Democracy: An Interview with Don Rothman."

The OWL at Purdue. http://owl.english.purdue.edu/owl/.

The OWL (Online Writing Lab) at Purdue Web site offers resources and comprehensive instruction on multiple topics of scholastic and professional writing including documenting electronic resources; MLA formatting and style guide; the writing process; creating a thesis statement; developing an outline; writing introductions, body paragraphs, and conclusions for argument papers and exploratory papers; invention presentations; prewriting; writing academic cover letters; action verbs; audience analysis; writing business; color theory presentation; writing cover letters;

designing an effective PowerPoint presentation; effective workplace writing; and many other topics.

Peoria Unified School District. http://staffweb.peoriaud.k12.az.us/SMHS_Library/CLASSES/LA/Persuasive.htm.
  This is a jackpot of persuasive writing resources at a multitude of levels. The topics include addressing both sides of controversial issues and writing persuasive arguments. Many links are provided, including links to a writing Handbook and how-tos. the Web site has

Prody, Kathleen, and Jean O'Connor "Persuasive Writing, Speaking, & Activities." www.hhs.helena.k12.mt.us/Teacherlinks/Oconnorj/persuasion.html.
  Prody and O'Connor developed this page in accordance with the American College Testing (ACT) writing assessment for juniors in Montana. The ACT organization was founded in 1959 and initially was a form of aptitude test and matchmaking service for prospective college students and the institutions. The options on the page include "Writing Prompts," "Links for Persuasive Writing and Speaking," "Lessons and Links for Persuasive Activities," and "Links to Handouts."

Rubrics and Self Assessment Project. Project Zero: Harvard Graduate School of Education. www.pz.harvard.edu/Research/RubricsSelfPE.htm.
  The persuasive essay rubric, developed by Heidi Goodrich Andrade of Project Zero, cites four categories for assessments of persuasive essays. The criteria to which the categories are applied are the claim, reasons in support of the claim, reasons against the claim, organization, voice and tone, word choice, sentence fluency, and conventions.

Shell, Jennifer. "Writing a Persuasive Essay." ALEX: Alabama Learning Exchange Web site. http://alex.state.al.us/lesson_view.php?id=16041.
  ALEX: The Alabama Learning Exchange is a Best of the Web: 2008 Digital Achievement Award page. Shell. a teacher at the Greenville High School in Butler County, Alabama, developed a lesson plan in which students research a variety of viewpoints on topics and write persuasively guided by the topics Shell identified, including recognizing fallacies in logic, developing critical thinking, and strengthening reading and writing skills. The lesson plan also included the evaluation of electronic media for "accuracy, appropriateness and bias." Shell recommends

that although the plan is designed for use primarily in English classes, the content could be adapted for social science and science classes.

Tarabia, Joanna. "Transitional Words and Phrases." University of Richmond Writing Center. http://writing2.richmond.edu/writing/wweb/trans1.html.

As the heading states, this page lists many useful transitional words and phrases.

Web English Teacher. "Argument & Persuasive Writing Lesson Plans and Learning Resources." www.webenglishteacher.com/argument.html.

This page provides lesson plans in many formats, including a variety of speeches to read and projects to initiate. The plans cover all grades, including high school.

WebQuest: The Power of Persuasive Writing. http://volweb.utk.edu/Schools/bedford/harrisms/mainpage.htm.

This Web site is separated into the categories of introduction, task, process, resources, roles, conclusion, and student gallery.

The Writing Centre of the University of British Columbia. "The Basic Principles of Persuasive Writing." www.writingcentre.ubc.ca/workshop/tools/argument.htm.

This page includes an introduction to the writing center and its writing workshop. Resources include "The Writer's Toolbox," which covers such topics as writing FAQs, effective titles, introductory paragraphs, thesis statements, development, unity and coherence, and conclusions.

YourDictionary.com. "Persuasiveness Quotes." www.yourdictionary.com/quotes/persuasiveness.

The title tells all: This Web page contains many quotes about persuasiveness.

Index

About the Author

CAROLYN DAVIS is a professional librarian, researcher, and specialist in development issues. She has also been a professional mediator. Davis is a graduate of the Simmons College Graduate School of Library and Information Science. The first Internet reference librarian at the Providence Athenaeum and past chair of the Resource Center at the Peace Corps headquarters in Jamaica, Davis was also a facilitator of the Jamaica Coalition on Disability. She has produced 27 publications and presentations in the United States, Britain, and Jamaica.